UNHOLY RAGE

By Lisa Cambria

TEACH Services, Inc.
P U B L I S H I N G
www.TEACHServices.com • (800) 367-1844

Copyright © 2016 Lisa Cambria

Copyright © 2016 TEACH Services, Inc.

ISBN-13: 978-1-4796-0697-9 (Paperback)

ISBN-13: 978-1-4796-0698-6 (ePub)

ISBN-13: 978-1-4796-0699-3 (Mobi)

Library of Congress Control Number: 2016905816

All Scripture is taken from the King James Version Bible. Public domain.

Published by

TEACH Services, Inc.
P U B L I S H I N G
www.TEACHServices.com • (800) 367-1844

Dedicated to the Holy Spirit who inspired the words of this book, and to my husband, Ed, who supported and encouraged me to continue this God-given assignment.

"That great dragon, the ancient serpent called the devil, or Satan who deceives the whole world, was cast out of heaven to the earth with all his angels."
(Rev 12:9)

"Your enemy, the devil, prowls around like a roaring lion looking for someone to devour. Resist him, standing firm in the faith…"
(1 Pet 5:8)

CHAPTER 1

David's heart pounds with a fear he's never known before. He blinks erratically, and then squeezes his eyes shut. Opening his eyes now, he attempts to focus his vision. Nothing. He stands in velvet blackness.

Suddenly David feels a stinging cold mass surround him. The ground beneath him is in upheaval and trembles with the sound of a thousand hoof beats. He loses his balance and falls to his hands and knees. With his head down, he whimpers in terror. The moist soil emanates a putrid stench of rotting carcasses. Suddenly, the ground ceases its quaking.

Now, there is dead stillness. He is unable to see anything. *Am I blind? Where am I?* He listens in the thick silence. Dread fills his mind as the smell of death fills his nostrils.

All of a sudden, David hears a creaking, cracking sound overhead, like that of a tree branch breaking in a windstorm. He crouches, covers his head with his arms, and waits for the branch to fall on him. Instead, he feels a hot, foul-smelling breath on the back of his neck from an animal that is nearly on top of him. He tries to back away, but it's as if the beast's breath contains a paralyzing agent. In complete darkness, he is filled with terror.

The unseen animal begins a low, rumbling snarl that changes to a malevolent snicker. David tries with all his might to get away as the demonic creature escalates its resounding voice to a mocking screech. The scream pierces his head like tiny daggers. Now he is able to thrash his arms to try to fend off this invisible threat to his soul. His hand hits something hard and cold. The screeching beast ceases its horrendous howls.

David opens his eyes, awakens and sits up in bed. He comes slowly to his senses. *It was that dream again.* He puts his hands over his face. *What's happening to me? Why am I having this nightmare over and over ever since…?* David can't bring himself to complete his thought.

After a moment, he stops trembling and examines his alarm clock; it's 7 a.m. He takes a deep breath to clear his mind of the all-too-real fear he has just been through. He thinks, *Hey! This is the last day of high school! Next year I'll be a senior!* Out loud, he mumbles to himself, "I can't wait to be a senior next year…and then on to college!"

His bedroom door is closed, but he hears Aunt Esther and his cousin Selah loudly discussing something that seems to be of importance to mother and daughter.

"Selah, why are you being so obstinate lately? Since you were six years old you've loved being in beauty pageants. You're beautiful, with those big green eyes and your long blonde hair. You stop everyone in their tracks every time you go on stage. No more arguing!" Esther continues, holding her hand up to Selah's face to hinder her daughter's objections. "We're going to Orlando this Saturday! Case closed!"

"But Mom, I'm going to the beach with Wes this Saturday. I'm not canceling another date with him. I'm crazy about him! Please don't make me go!"

"Selah Rose, this is important for your future career. The appointments for your hair and dress fitting are set, and I've spent a lot of money on you already. I'm not going to allow you to jeopardize your chances of being discovered at this open audition for a new movie because of a boy. Now go put on your cheerleading outfit for school."

Selah's pleading doesn't work. She knows that she's lost when her mother uses her middle name. She sighs in defeat and stomps off upstairs. *I'll show her; I'm not going to be on the cheerleading squad next year! I don't want to hang with all those "Miss Goody-Two-Shoes" anyway!*

Esther sits down at the kitchen table as she listens to her daughter trod up the steps. She is sympathetic to Selah's attitude. She herself had once been a beauty queen with offers of modeling and acting at the age of 17, but she had been careless with Selah's father, John Abrams. She had gotten pregnant and married out of high school, giving up her chance at wealth and fame.

My looks and talent were wasted on marriage and motherhood. Now it's too late; I'm almost 34, with two daughters, and to top it off, a nephew to care for. John's brother got himself and his wife killed in a car accident two years ago and David came to live with us. He had no one else. It's not fair! Why has life been so rotten for me? I have to keep Selah from making the same mistake I made, one that I will regret for the rest of my life. The only good thing I have going for me is that my husband is the mayor of Rocky Water, Florida, she thinks with a prideful smirk on her face.

At that moment, Esther's 7-year-old daughter, Josephine, comes into the kitchen, followed closely by David, who stands in the doorway while Josie joyfully runs to her mother.

"Hi Mommy! I'm all ready for school. David helped me pick out something to wear for the last day of school." Her bright brown eyes produce a small frown of confusion. "Why don't you ever help me pick something out anymore? I like having David here with us, don't you, Mommy?"

Esther simply looks at David as she rises from the table and places her empty coffee cup in the sink. "Did you brush your hair and teeth, Josephine?" Esther asks with her back to her daughter.

"Yep, David and I shared the bathroom sink to do our teeth and hair together while you and Selah were talking. Can Jane Wilson watch me when you and Selah go to Orlando? She plays games with me and reads books and lets me go in the pool with her. Can she watch me again, huh? Please, Mommy?"

Esther snaps, "Well, of course, Josie. Who else would put up with your incessant jabbering?"

"YAY! I'm gonna go in and see Daddy before school!"

While Esther continues to stand at the sink, David follows Josie out of the kitchen. He sits on the sofa in the living room while Josie runs into the den to see her father.

Why is Aunt Esther mad all of the time? David wonders. *Probably because I'm here; I'm angry too, at you God,* he thinks as he looks to the ceiling, *for letting my parents die and my friend Stephen be murdered, but I don't talk to a little kid like she does. Josie's too sweet to yell at.* Josie blurts out with blissful honesty whatever is on her mind at any time. David realizes that he has grown quite fond of her over the past two years. He has no siblings, so he thoroughly enjoys the closeness he shares with his two cousins and Uncle John. *I wish that Aunt Esther would love me.*

Because Josie had flung the door to the den wide open, David is able to hear everything being said in his uncle's office. The joyful perkiness in Josie's voice never ceases to amaze David.

Josie jumps up on her father's lap where he sits behind his desk. She asks, "What are you gonna do today, Daddy?"

"I'm meeting with engineers to discuss how to fix Annie on Dragon Point."

With concern in her voice, Josie asks, "What's wrong with her? What are engineers?"

As David overhears their conversation, he remembers that Annie is the name that the townspeople affectionately call a concrete and steel sculpture of a dragon which stands on the southern tip of Merritt Island, two miles off the east coast of Florida. Annie had been featured in a magazine for sailboarders a few years ago, so she is known nationwide by the fun-loving group who participate in the sport. David's attention turns back to the conversation in the den.

"Engineers are people who know all about buildings and structures like Annie. They'll take a look at her to see what repairs are needed so she doesn't blow down in a bad storm. The artist who made her would be the best person for the job, but he died a few years ago."

"Make her better, OK, Daddy? She has four babies to take care of. Let's see…their names are Sunshine, Joy, Charity, and Hope. Yep! That's their names. Bye!" Josie gives her father a kiss on the cheek, hops off of his lap and runs out to the living room. "My bus is here!" She gives David a hug and picks up her backpack. With her long, golden brown hair flowing behind her, she runs to the front door and yells, "Bye, Mommy!"

In the den, John has his right elbow on the desk, slowly rubbing his chin, deep in thought.

David approaches the open door to the den, notices that his uncle looks busy, and is about to turn around when John sees him.

"David! Come in."

David sits down in a large plush armchair facing the desk.

As John leans back in his chair he says, "Josie sure likes the dragon. I do too. I grew up here in Rocky Water, and it's been over on the island as long as I can remember." With a pensive crease in his brow he states, "Have I told you the history of Annie yet?"

"No."

"Well, she's 35 feet tall and 65 feet long, and as you have probably noticed, she's green. Legend says that an Indian witch doctor conjured her up to protect his people from the fierce tribes here on the mainland. In reality, an artist sculpted it. It has a door to its hollow interior, and a staircase up the neck where you can peer out of the nostrils. The belly was once a playhouse for the owner's son."

David simply smiles casually because he and his friends use the dragon on a regular basis for their "meetings."

John continues. "I remember that every Fourth of July, the townspeople gathered in Pineapple Park next to the library, directly across the Indian River Lagoon from Annie, and watched fire shoot out of her mouth and smoke billow out of her nostrils." David notices a sparkle of nostalgia in his uncle's faraway look. "Oh well, those days are over. I want to get it reinforced before it collapses." Realizing then that David had come to him, John asks, "Was there something you wanted to discuss?"

David exudes a long sigh. "Do you think that Aunt Esther is all right with me living here?"

John takes a deep breath and leans forward with his elbows on the desk. "David, I think that she's just wrapped up in racing back and forth to Orlando for Selah and all of the preparations that girls feel they must do. She's very busy with fundraisers for the city as the mayor's wife. She's always been a perfectionist. Maybe she's trying too hard and is worn out most of the time. Believe me, she's always cranky when she's exhausted."

"OK. Thanks, Uncle John," David says as he rises from the chair, not convinced of his uncle's explanation of his aunt's distant behavior toward him. "I'm going to see if Selah is ready to walk to school."

"I've got to leave soon, too. I don't want to be late for this meeting," adds John as he gathers his papers from his desk and places them in his briefcase.

"I'll see you for dinner tonight, Uncle John."

Selah is descending the staircase as David enters the living room. He perceives her tension and frustration. Quietly he says, "Hey, don't let your mom get to you so much." As he has many times before, he distorts his face with tongue outstretched in an attempt to make his cousin laugh. He thinks he detects a slight up-turn at the corners of her mouth.

"Let's go, clown head," Selah retorts with affection.

David thinks to himself, *I guess that's as close to a smile that I'm going to get out of her. I wonder what she did with her bad moods before I got here? She probably stewed and boiled over until she vented to her fellow cheerleaders.* David has learned to keep quiet until they were out of the house. Then he tries to lighten her mood with funny stories about when he was first learning to surf at Cocoa Beach many years ago.

It is Selah who first speaks this morning. "I've been thinking. Mom says that cheerleading presents a more prestigious résumé for pageants and movie auditions. Well, I'll show her," she snorts arrogantly. "I'm not going to be on the squad next year. Today is the last day of our junior year of high school, and it's the very last day I'm wearing this outfit I have on," she proclaims with a sense of victorious pride.

David doesn't know what to say about that, but instead informs her of the conversation he heard between his uncle and Josie.

They arrive at school ten minutes before the first bell.

CHAPTER 2

The moment that Selah joins the other cheerleaders near the front steps of the school, she tells them of her argument with her mother. David sees Daniel Windfeather and his gang of friends. He thinks, *I know they're a bunch of miscreants, and I know that I'm going to eventually get in trouble, so I don't know why I hang out with them.* Deep down inside, David feels comfortable and well liked by them, unlike his relationship with his aunt.

The group of boys greets David with smiles and back-slapping, attention his aunt never gives him. He likes Daniel. The two of them often get together to play video games after school and on weekends. They meet on Friday nights with Selah at Dragon Point. On Saturday nights, the three of them, and sometimes Josie, go to Rocky Water Speedway, which is owned by Daniel's father.

David pulls Daniel aside to give him the news about the work to be done on Annie.

"Rats!" responds Daniel. "We can't let our meeting place be discovered. It's a perfect hideout, hidden behind that empty old house on the point." For a moment he is deep in thought and then adds, "We get out at noon today. Then we'll go to the dragon, load our things in my dad's truck, and take them to my house."

Meanwhile, Selah watches Jane Wilson, a small, slightly overweight classmate, approach the front steps near where the cheerleading squad is standing.

Donna Preston, co-captain with Selah, says, "I like Jane. She's smart and always in a good mood. It's kind of nice to know someone who isn't always complaining about something or someone. And to think; her brother Stephen was just murdered back in the fall."

The other girls glance over at Selah, who is glaring at Donna. Donna's creamy milk chocolate skin turns deep pink around her cheeks.

Changing the subject quickly, Donna asks cheerfully, "Selah, your cousin David is cute, with his curly blond hair and big shoulders; and he's such a good surfer. Does he ever ask about me?"

Selah is surprised at the intensity of anger that seethes inside her right now. Her bad mood reaches a pinnacle. Her heart pounds with such rage that she feels as though her carotid artery will burst.

Jane sits down on the steps nearby and becomes the object of Selah's rage. Selah steps toward Jane and snarls, "Mind your own business!" as she viciously flails at her hapless victim's pile of papers on her lap. Papers take to the air and begin to blow all around. Jane's eyes fill with confused surprise as Selah's eyes fill with fury.

"Selah!" admonishes Donna as she approaches Jane, whose face is frozen in astonishment.

Jane begins to gather her far-flung notes. Selah giggles and bounds up the steps, followed by the other girls.

Donna utters a sound of exasperation as she looks into Jane's eyes, but then follows Selah up the steps and in the front door.

Later that day, it's almost noon, and Jane sits down outside on the top step of the sun-drenched landing of the school's front door. The final bell of her junior year will soon ring, announcing to all of Rocky Water the beginning of summer vacation. With anticipation of her plan for the next three months, she lifts her face to the bright overhead sun, closes her eyes, and takes a deep breath of the warm humid air of late May.

When she opens her eyes, she sees a swallow-tail butterfly float in front of her and flutter over the low wall on either side of the wide stair-case. Instantly, a memory of a year earlier comes to her mind. It was of her and her mother in Pineapple Park.

Overhead had been a flawless blue sky that afternoon, fading to pastel at the horizon beyond Dragon Point. Jane and her mother, Faith, had both been pleasantly relaxed when they had left the library to sit down on

a bench overlooking the Indian River lagoon. They surveyed their surroundings and breathed in the fresh air of early spring. As Faith raised her
eyes to the newly budding trees, she told Jane of the wonderful miraculous
power that lay behind nature and all of its creatures.

That day long ago, Faith had reminded Jane that she had always loved
butterflies. "When you were three years old, you loved to blow the milk-
weeds that grew here in the park in the summer. You'd chase after the
floating seeds and the butterflies in the air. Oh, how you loved butterflies
flittering around. You were fascinated with them."

Now, as Jane sits in the sun on the steps, the butterfly once again
shows itself. She gets up, descends the stairs to watch where it goes, and
she rounds the edge of the low wall on her right. She spots it in the tall
bushes against the cement wall of the building. Feeling joyful and adven-
turous, she makes her way into the back part of the garden and kneels
down in the mulch under the tall bushes to be nearer to the butterfly.
Suddenly, the bell rings as the front doors open to release the students
from their "prison."

Amid the cacophony of noise, Jane hears Selah's voice above it all.
"Awesome, Mr. Potiphar! I'm learning a lot of cool stuff from your books
in our meetings."

Jane realizes that she cannot be seen over the wall where she crouches.
She decides to remain quietly in place, where she unintentionally eaves-
drops.

"Well, I'm glad to hear that," Mr. Potiphar replies. "And I'm pleased that
you bring friends that you can trust to our secret meetings. These lessons are
only for those who have certain beliefs and special abilities. The effective-
ness of the meetings would be hindered by anyone who doesn't believe and
would interfere before you and the others have perfected your powers."

"Right, Mr. Potiphar. We know. We've kept it secret for six months
now, since you invited us. No outsider will find out from one of us what
we're doing. I'm very careful about who I choose to join us."

"Good! I knew I could depend on you. Don't forget, Thursday next
week is full moon."

"Our usual? The shack at Canova Beach? I'm bringing two that night."

"Who?" asked Mr. Potiphar.

"My cousin David, and Daniel Windfeather."

"Great choices, my dear! Your boyfriend, Wes, won't be the only boy
then."

Jane hears their voices trail off as they descend the stairs and walk
away from her and her hiding place.

CHAPTER 3

Jane sighs with relief for not being caught eavesdropping. Curious, she stands and makes her way out of the garden, thinking, *special abilities? Powers? Something weird is going on and I'm going to find out what it is!*

Jane is startled by a familiar voice behind her. Turning around, she sees Josie, who has come from the elementary school next door. Jane waves at Josie's teacher to assure her that the child is taken care of. In her excitement about school being out for the summer, Josie has run over to the high school under the watchful eye of her teacher.

"Ain't it awesome that we get out at the same time today, Jane?"

"Yes, it is," replies Jane as she gives the child her attention. She will think about what to do, if anything, about the conversation she has just overheard.

With a mischievous look in her eyes, Josie takes Jane by the hand and blurts out, "I have a secret that I've been saving for our last day of school."

Jane's mind is somewhere else temporarily. "Did you see Adam? My brother is always late." Then she realizes what Josie said. "A secret, huh? What is it?"

"I'll show you. Come on!" entices Josie as they begin the walk home.

Ten minutes later, they pass by Josie's house to Jane's house next door. Jane asks, "Don't you want to go to your house instead of mine?"

"No, the secret thing is in your house. I found it awhile ago and kept it a secret until now! I was sad all over again when I found it, but now it's time to show it to you."

Jane unlocks the door. Josie runs into the living room and opens the cabinet under the entertainment center. She reaches in the back, pulls out a maroon, fabric-covered notebook with gold braiding, and holds it out to Jane.

Jane stares with unbelief. *It's not possible! I thought I had dreamed that it had happened!* Again she is pulled back in time six months ago when, after Stephen, her older brother, had been killed, she was sitting out on her front porch mourning his death.

She had been staring blankly across the street from where she sat on the porch. It was nearly dark and a chill had begun in the October evening. She sat motionless. Fatigue made her eyes heavy. She took long, slow breaths of the cool air as it softly slinked around her. Lowering her head and closing her eyes, she had said aloud to herself, "Why? I don't understand. Why Stephen?" Fatigue had finally overcome her when she was startled awake by a man and woman who were standing on the front walkway to the house.

There had been a full moon and Jane was chilled.

"I'm sorry. Please don't be frightened," the woman had said in a soft, pleasant voice. "We wanted to bring this to you." Then she walked up to Jane on the porch.

Jane had been groggy and fuzzy-headed as the woman held out a fabric notebook closed with a zipper. Jane had squinted her eyes in confusion. There was light coming from the living room window, giving the strange woman's face a glowing lambency. As Jane slowly reached out to take the notebook, she looked into the soft eyes of this gentle stranger. Her eyes were pale aqua and sparkled like sunlight on water.

She smiled tenderly as Jane accepted the mysterious gift. She looked at the notebook. It was a rich maroon color with gold trim. On the front was embroidered in gold thread the words, "Children Walking in Truth."

When Jane looked up again, the couple was walking away. "Thank you," she yelled after them, still in a state of drowsy confusion. They had turned toward her and gave a slight wave of their hands. She watched as they stepped off of the curb onto the quiet street and disappeared before her eyes. *Was it a dream? They vanished into thin air!*[1]

"Jane," Josie startles her out of her reverie. "Take it. It's OK. Stephen left this for us."

Jane, still in shock, slowly reaches out to take the notebook. "I... I... didn't think this was real. I thought it had been a dream. Where did you find it?"

"Under this chair," Josie replies. "Your dad's chair."

Tenderly, Josie takes Jane by the hand and leads her over to the sofa to sit down. Jane sits still for only a moment, but Josie is full of excitement about sharing her secret. Josie takes the notebook carefully from Jane and unzips around the fabric. Then she slowly gives it back to Jane.

Jane's hands shake as she takes the maroon-covered notebook. Tears fog Jane's eyesight. Hatred for the boy who killed her brother grips at her heart. Josie gently squeezes Jane's arm. Tears begin to well up in Josie's eyes also at the sight of her friend's face.

"It's alright," Josie assures her. Looking into Jane's hate-filled eyes brimming over with tears, Josie slowly takes the notebook from Jane's hands. "Whenever you think you're ready, I'll be here," Josie expresses with empathy.

Jane, however, forces a smile and wipes away her tears. Seeing the tears in Josie's eyes, she consoles her young friend with, "I'm sad all over again, too, but it's all right. I'm glad that you showed this to me, but I loathe that boy and the way I feel every time I think about..."

Just then, Faith comes home unexpectedly. "Mom, what are you doing home so early from work?"

"Adam!" With joyous enthusiasm, Josie runs to give Adam an adoring embrace.

"I took off in order to pick up Adam from junior high school. Your little brother here has been getting in trouble so much lately that I wanted to make sure he follows the rules that I set last night for his grounding." With exasperation in her voice she adds, "You know, as a social worker, I spend all day with families that have major problems, and I'm going to nip *this* one in the bud." Josie isn't sure who Faith is talking to.

Jane can see that her little brother is humiliated. Faith turns Adam around with her hand on her son's shoulder and points him to his room without saying a word.

Josie returns to the cabinet and places the notebook back in the cabinet while Faith has her back turned. "Now you can look at it whenever you're ready," she says quietly to Jane. "I'll read it with you if you want me to, because I've read through some of it already. Do you want to come over to my house now?"

Jane acquires her composure by taking a deep breath and squaring her shoulders.

"Yes," she tells Josie. "Hey, Mom?" Jane yells to her mother, who had walked to the kitchen, "I'm taking Josie home to babysit until her mom gets home."

"OK. Bye, Josie," they hear coming from the kitchen.

CHAPTER 4

Three days later, Jane is grateful that she has the house to herself. Her parents are at work, and she doesn't have to pick up Josie at 3:30 from the recreation center where she takes baton lessons, because Esther has asked Selah to pick up her little sister. Jane looks over at the cabinet under the TV, but turns away. Instead, she picks up Pasquale, her cat, and takes him to the kitchen to give him his afternoon snack.

She decides to take her iPod to her favorite spot in the woods in Pineapple Park, a short distance from her house, where she often goes to be alone.

As she steps down the embankment to the small creek in the park, lizards scurry from their places, as if annoyed by the interruption. A large dark brown male stays nearby. The bright red flap of skin under his chin moves in and out as he watches Jane sit down, cross-legged, on the grass among the wildflowers.

She loves these times to herself at her place in the woods as much as she loves to sing. For as long as she can remember she's been in the choirs, both at school and church.

The sun is slightly behind her. It feels pleasantly warm on her head and toasty on her back. The breeze blows through her short, curly hair. She begins to sing along with the music, not caring if anyone hears.

Selah is mad at Wes for canceling their date this evening, so David convinces her to take a walk with him to feed the horses that many people own in this part of town. Because of her affinity for horses, David has discovered that this is the only way her temper can be cooled when she gets angry. "If Wes would rather hang with his friends, then, *fine*! I'm not going to sit around and sulk," she replies to David's suggestion.

Today, after feeding the horses a special treat she brought from home for them, Selah and David wander further than usual, and they run into Daniel Windfeather.

As the trio walks on the sidewalk, Selah listens to the boys talk about their favorite computer games.

"…Yeah, and there's blood flyin' everywhere…" exclaims Daniel.

Selah imagines Daniel as a knight who will defend her honor in spite of Wes. Then her attention drifts back to Daniel and David as they speak of the books about a boy and wizard school.

"…and wouldn't it be awesome to have one of those cloaks that could make me invisible?" asks Daniel. "I could sneak around and no one could see me. I could scare the daylights out of them! And the spell to disarm my enemies…I would go for the kill. I don't care that the spell is forbidden; I'd use it anyway." [1]

David adds, "I'd want to be able to control people so they would do whatever I'd tell them to do. That would be awesome to have the seductive powers like those in that book about the good vampires who sparkle in the sunlight."

"My enemies would be at my mercy…and I wouldn't give them any!" Daniel asserts with a stabbing action. Like a victorious gladiator, he raises his arms over his head and imitates the sound of a cheering crowd. David cheers along with Daniel for a moment, then changes the subject by reminding them that work on Annie has been delayed.

"We can go ahead and move our things back into the dragon. The plans for reinforcement have been postponed. Let's get back to holding séances and using the Ouija board inside Annie to conjure up spirits who'll do our bidding," David suggests excitedly.

"I like doing that stuff too." Selah continues, "Harry learns to use the power that's already in him to cast spells because he's special, not like ordinary humans who don't have access to special powers. Wait until Thursday night when we go to the haunted beach cabin and see what Mr. Potiphar does. It's exciting to learn the things he teaches."

"Yeah, but wouldn't it be awesome to cast a spell and get everything you want?" David continues, "How about we meet in Annie tomorrow?"

Selah is about to agree with him when, suddenly, they hear someone singing off in the distance. They glance at each other with matching curiosity on their faces.

"C'mon," says Daniel, "Let's see where that's coming from!"

"It's probably someone playing a CD," concludes David.

"But there's no music!" conveys Daniel.

"Then it's a capella," announces Selah, "a song without any accompanying music."

"It's coming from this way," Daniel states with certainty, pointing to the left. He heads into the wooded area, leaving the sidewalk. David extends his arm toward the woods, indicating that Selah should precede him.

Selah observes the intensity with which Daniel hunts for the perplexing and enthralling voice they hear. She listens with envy to the intonation of clear notes being sung with unwavering lilt. The sound of the girl's voice is captivating.

"There!" whispers Daniel as he points.

Selah and David follow his pointed finger to the girl sitting cross-legged on the ground across the brook. *She looks familiar,* thinks Selah.

Daniel decides that the singing girl has not heard them. They are well hidden behind some large palmetto bushes where they have crouched upon spying her.

The small girl has her face turned upward. Her eyes are closed and her hands are holding the earpieces. She gently sways side to side as her voice resounds through the woods. The words are beautiful and the resonance of her voice penetrates Selah's heart.

David interrupts Selah's moment of amazement. "Let's go scare the living daylights out of her," he demands. "That's a freaky thing to be doing, and she needs to learn a lesson."

As he moves to stand up, Selah pulls on his arm. "No! Listen!" she demands in a stage whisper. "Her voice is amazing! I thought I could sing, but…she doesn't have her glasses on, but I think it's Jane Wilson!"

Daniel and David stare in amazement. Selah puts her finger to her mouth in a gesture to keep them quiet so she can hear the words.

Once again, David disturbs Selah's focus of concentration on the words. "Oh, man, this is a religious gospel song, and it's freakin' me out. I say that we sneak up on her from behind, grab her and throw her in the creek. It ain't deep."

"Leave her alone, David," Daniel orders as he recalls Selah's rancor toward Jane on the last day of school. "Why is everyone mean to her? She's always nice to me."

"Shhh!" orders Selah.

Suddenly, Jane stops singing and removes her earpieces. She replaces her glasses and stands to stretch with warm contentment. She wipes the beads of perspiration from her forehead and turns to climb the slight incline of the embankment to return home.

As she takes the first step, Jane hears rustling in the bushes across the brook. She turns to look at the spot she thinks the noise has come from. *It must be male lizards fighting over a female.* She briefly watches the pattern of the wandering patches of light undulating through the overhead branches like silver ribbons in the soft breeze.

As she turns around to go, she thinks she spots some vague shadows behind the large palmetto bushes across the brook. The swaying, muted shadows from the overhead branches gently stroke the forest floor as the sun sparkles off the water in the brook.

Jane glances around her spot in the woods, mesmerized by the splendor of light and shadows that dance and shift among the bushes and wildflowers. The tiny flowers glimmer in and out in the afternoon sun and shadows as if the blossoms were made of shimmering crystals. A saying she has heard from her mother flashes through her mind: *"See how the lilies of the field grow…not even Solomon in all his splendor was dressed like one of these."* [2]

Lilies have been her favorite flower since that afternoon a long time ago with her father in her grandfather's garden. As soon as she had set her eyes on the array of yellow flowers with chiffon-like daintiness, she had pulled her hand out of her mother's and had whisked on her cherubic feet over to the garden of exquisite colors. *The plants were tall!* she remembers, but not so tall that she couldn't stand on tiptoes to touch the tender and delicate blooms with their uneven, feathered edges. They seemed to bow down to her in the gentle wind. She viewed the mixture of orange patches softly blended with the yellow hue. In her fascination, her young eyes glistened with illumination. She then felt the warmth of her father's arms gently hug her as he softly kissed her head. She turned to his welcoming arms and tender eyes with enthusiasm.

"Look at these large green leaves, Janie," her daddy had said.

She reluctantly turned away from her father's eyes as he took her diminutive hand gently between his large and powerful fingers. He had slowly traced her tiny index finger down the satiny leaves that gently curved upward, as if they also wished to be near the beauty of the unfolding blossoms.

To Jane's small stature, the stately plants with sinewy stalks seemed to lightly brush the clouds. She gazed up at their loftiness against the sky. Her father stood up slowly to reach a height far above the tallest lily. He held out his hand and said, "Follow me."

Jane gladly slipped her hand into his. With much effort, she tried to match his every step on the narrow path through the garden. She recalled that she had to be careful not to let her feet slip off of each large white stone into the moist, rich soil where the lilies grew as she tried to match her father's steps. She squeezed his hand tightly as she listened to him speak.

"These flowers grew from one bulb. All of these lilies are from one single bulb, planted on the day you were born. As the plant sprouted and grew, it extended a part of itself in the darkness underground to start another sprout, which in turn reached up to the light of the sun. Then this new seedling, once it was grown up, extended its own arms out so that another could be started and struggle its way to the surface in search of the light. So, this whole garden was begun with one bulb. Isn't that amazing!"

Jane spotted something in the garden, which drew her attention away from the lilies. She ran to it, leaving her father's grasp.

"Don't touch that. It's bad and it'll hurt you," but Jane had not listened. She stroked the thorn under the dead, brown stalk which had no blossoms, and pricked her finger.

"Ow, Daddy, I'm bleeding." She looked back to the white stones, which seemed to glisten with brightness through her tears. Then she watched as her father bent down and beckoned her to come to him. She rushed into his arms and hugged his neck. He embraced her with strong arms, lifted her up and held her tightly.

"I'm never gonna let go again, Daddy," she had whispered as she clung to his neck. "Will you carry me inside so I can sit on your lap?"

"Well of course, sweetie," he replied with a smile. He cuddled her frail body against his chest and murmured, "Always and forever."

For the rest of the way, he had carried her on the path toward the gate that opened to the front door of his father's house.

With a sad smile, Jane has not recalled this memory until now, standing in these woods. She slowly turns and heads for home, forgetting about the noise from across the small brook.

"Whew!" David exclaims, wiping perspiration from his forehead. "I thought maybe she could see us. She stood there a long time just staring. She is *so* weird."

"I've known her since sixth grade," says Selah. "We've never been friends. We had a lot of classes together, even this past year in school, but I never knew she could sing like *that!* She's always been so shy and quiet. Josie sure likes her, though. Oh no! What time is it? I've got to pick up Josie at 3:30!"

"We can go to the speedway and borrow my dad's truck," offers Daniel.

"Thanks, Daniel. That would be great. Josie will be excited about riding in your truck with us."

They have thirty minutes to get to the truck and reach Josie on time.

CHAPTER 5

"All right, is everyone ready?" asks Daniel, once they are all seated in their own chosen spots in the belly of the dragon at Dragon Point the next day.

"Hey!" Wes blurts out suddenly. "Why do you always get to lead? Doesn't anyone else get a chance?" Selah adores Wes's angular jaw line, his dark wavy hair and large brown eyes as he challenges Daniel, their leader.

"Well, I know how to get the spirits' attention. I know the nuances of séances, you might say," responds Daniel with a confident smile. "But, if someone else would like to lead this session, be my guest."

Wes cocks his head and purses his lips. "Nah, that's OK. I was merely curious." He then picks up the planchette of the Ouija board and examines the heart-shaped piece of plastic with a window, turning it over. "I wonder how this thing works anyway. What makes it move when we barely touch it?"

"There are many ghosts around us all the time," Daniel answers with an air of authority, "but we can't see them. A Ouija board allows the living souls --- *us* --- to communicate with the souls of the dead, by letting them know that we want to talk to them. They can tell us things which benefit us, and they love telling the secrets of the spirit world to us by spelling out the answers to our questions. They make the thing we place our fingers on, the planchette, move."

"It sure is awesome," Wes adds. He places the planchette, which lies on the floor in the center of the circle, back on the board.

"OK, go ahead, Master of the Spirit World," Wes jokes affectionately. About ten minutes later…

"Are you male or female?" Selah asks the unseen entity moving the planchette.

F-E-M-A-L-E

"Where were you when you died?"

U-T-A-H

"How did you die?"

G-U-N

"Who killed you?"

A-D-O-C-T-O-R H-I-D-G-U-N-I-N-G-L-O-B-E-I-N-O-F-F-I-C-E.[1]

Everyone was very excited at the end of the half-hour session. "Wasn't that awesome?" Daniel exclaims. "That dead girl answered all of our questions. The four of us seem to have special abilities together to bring the spirits around. But, you know what I've decided?" Daniel didn't wait for anyone to inquire about what decision he had made.

"I think we need a secretary to take notes of our meetings; we need to write down all the letters so we can better understand longer answers. What do you guys think?"

No one answers.

Daniel continues, "I think that's a good idea; and I have someone in mind." He doesn't tell them immediately, drawing the others' attention completely.

"Let's invite her to be part of our group by asking for her…" Daniel searches for the right word, "expert help." He intentionally lingers on the moment hoping for a positive response from the others.

"Well, who?" Selah demands impatiently.

Impishly he smiles. "Jane Wilson."

Meanwhile, Jane is at home. She sits and stares at the cabinet which contains the notebook when the phone rings.

"Hello?"

"Hi, Jane, it's Mrs. Abrams. Can you do me a big favor, spur of the moment?"

"Sure. What is it?"

"We have a major issue at the Garden Club and they called for my help. Are you able to watch Josie now? She wants to come over there. Is that all right with you? I shouldn't be very long. She would get bored if I took her to my meeting."

"That's fine. I don't mind. Send her right over, Mrs. A."

Actually, Jane is grateful for the company. Josie is one of her closest friends, she realizes. *That's very sad when the only friends I have are Josie and Adam. Josie is more mature than other seven-year-olds.* Adam is still confined to his room until tomorrow when his grounding is over. Faith had made Jane promise not to let Adam out of his room. Thankfully, he has behaved for the week.

All of a sudden, the front door opens and in runs Josie. Immediately, Jane gets a giant bear hug and a barrage of questions.

"Are we alone now? Do you want to read the notebook with me? Have you opened it yet? I think Stephen was an awesome person, don't you?"

Jane is surprised with herself that she is in shock at Josie's exuberance over the notebook, an exuberance for which Jane is grateful. *I think I can open it now that she's here. Josie adored Stephen as much as I did.*

Josie stands with her hands clasped in front of her. Her head is cocked to one side with an inquisitive expression while she waits for Jane's answer.

Again Jane is thankful, because Josie isn't pushing her into something for which she may not be ready. *But I am ready. I want to read what Stephen wrote.*

"OK. Go get it."

Slowly, a reaffirming smile crosses Josie's face. She takes Jane's hands in hers and says, "We'll go slowly. That's what I had to do, and it makes it easier. But first, I want to tell you that there's nothing bad in there, only good things that he discovered."

Josie runs to the cabinet and retrieves the notebook. Butterflies are invading Jane's stomach as Josie sits down next to her on the couch and carefully unzips the maroon notebook. "OK, are you ready?"

Jane holds her breath for a moment, and then nods her head in answer to the question.

"I'll read it to you if you want me to," suggests Josie with compassion.

Again, Jane nods her head without making a sound.

The first page contains the words: *The Secret Kingdom* by Pat Robertson, published in 1992:[2]

Underneath this was printed the page number, 32, followed by the words:

As self-restraint and regard for God rapidly diminish under the assault of secular humanism (which is the acceptance of all beliefs and lifestyles spoken of in "politically correct" terms), "Judges are less inclined to make decisions based on the Bible" and "The Constitution is what the judges say it is..." In other words, in order to please the majority of people, God's message to the world has been forgotten. The Biblical principles on which our government and its Constitution were originally based have become outlawed in society. (Paraphrased). The second *Humanist Manifesto* of 1973 lawfully denied "'The existence of a supernatural God who hears and answers prayers.'" (pg 34).

Over the years, this opinion has spread to a majority of people practicing hedonism, "doing their own thing", and "If it feels good, do it," (pg 34), which in turn has led to a record number of cases of mental breakdowns and suicides, perhaps because those who do not know Jesus still have an empty sadness within themselves. This void of sadness cannot be filled with material things or sensual pleasures. This empty space is a longing for total fulfillment and happiness, a space which can only be satisfied by God because He planned it that way.

Josie looks at Jane with confusion in her eyes. "I don't understand everything, but it seems that Stephen might have been sad about our government when he wrote this part. You know how much he loved history and politics."

"It almost sounds like he was doing research and added his own thoughts, like a term paper for school," adds Jane.

"Jane, the empty space in everybody, is it in the heart?"

"Yes, I think so. My heart hurt when Stephen died. I feel empty and sad, even now, like something is missing."

Josie ponders a moment, and then asks, "Is it the same feeling I get after I'm tired of a new toy and there's an empty feeling because I'm bored with it? I always want to get something new so that I'll be happy again."

"Yeah, it's kinda like that. Stephen said that material things, like toys or pretty dresses, won't keep a person happy for very long. Only God can."

Unknown to the two girls, Faith had returned and overheard their conversation. At first, she wants to run out there with them to look at the notebook her son has left, but she decides that her impulsive action would be the wrong thing to do. With tears in her eyes, she listens to the two of them converse on a subject which she has not heard before from them.

"But, how can we reach high enough to talk to God?" asks Josie. Then, with excitement in her voice and eyes, she blurts out, "If we go to the highest mountain in the world, we can!"

Faith thinks quietly to herself, *I once felt that emptiness too, but it's not as bad as it had first been. I know why my void isn't empty anymore. It's time I talk to my old friend Esther. But first, it's the right time for Adam to hear what I have to say.*

CHAPTER 6

On Thursday morning, Jane decides to find out what time the full moon will rise tonight. Since she overheard that strange conversation on the last day of school a week ago, her curiosity has taken a strong hold on her imagination.

I know! I'll look up the phone number to the weather station. Rocky Water is the home of the county's radar weather forecasting office. They'll know what time the full moon will rise tonight.

When she realizes that the address is nearby, Jane decides to ride her bike there instead of calling. She is curious to see what a radar station looks like.

It was a 10 minute ride on her bicycle to the station, which she discovers sits on the east side of a dead end road. Across the street, Jane sees a home for runaway and displaced girls. ***The Hacienda Girls' Ranch***, the sign reads.

She spots a girl sitting in a rocking chair on the front porch of the small building. The girl is very pregnant and smoking a cigarette. She stares at Jane with a sad look on her face.

Jane smiles slightly, parks her bike and turns to enter the weather station. The man inside greets her with a friendly smile.

"Hi there, young lady. What can I do for you?"

"I need to find out what time the moon rises tonight. Can you help me?"

"Certainly can. Wait here, I'll be right back."

He returns with a computer printout which contains statistical information such as rainfall and record highs for each day of the month of June going back to 1950. He had circled the information she had requested.

Jane thanks him and walks out into the bright sunlight. She looks over to where she had seen the pregnant girl. The girl is gone, and so is her bicycle!

Jane stands in place with unbelief at what has just happened. *I was inside for only a couple of minutes!* She glances around and looks for her bike. *It's really gone! Should I call the police?*

She heaves a deep sigh and begins to walk home as she folds the paper to fit into the pocket of her shorts. *Did that girl steal my bike?*

With sheer luck, Jane spots the girl on her bike on the cross street where there are many houses. The girl is pulling into a driveway three houses down on the right.

Jane crosses the street quickly, nears the side of the first house on the right, and peeks around the corner. Suddenly, a tall dark haired boy appears. Jane blinks with disbelief. *It's Daniel Windfeather!* Then she sees David Abrams! *I can't believe it!*

Daniel hands something to the pregnant girl and takes the bike. It appears as if the girl were counting money. *She stole my bike and sold it!*

Jane leans against the house, uncertain as to what to do next. She closes her eyes in exasperation, when suddenly a Scripture that her mother had taught her comes to mind, something about when someone takes what is yours, don't demand it back, don't condemn them, but forgive them.[1]

She hangs her head at the loss of her bicycle, but feels relief that she receives an answer as to what to do about her situation. Tears come to her eyes as she slowly turns toward home and thinks, *I have to find out what they do in that shack at Canova Beach!*

By the time she reaches her front door, she makes the decision to call in a report to the police, but not to implicate Daniel or David in the incident.

After telling the desk officer what happened, he responds, "Yeah, we've had a bike theft ring for about two years now. There's not too much I can do to get your bike back, but what you can do is to come to our storage facility behind the station on Apollo Boulevard once a week to see if it's been brought in. We think that kids steal the bikes and then sell them to the ringleader, but he rejects some of them, so we find them in ditches or in the woods. So far we've had no leads to follow up on. Sorry."

Feeling dejected, Jane hangs up the phone, leans back in her father's chair and sighs. *Well, at least I know a little about what's going on; the girl probably needs the money. No wonder Daniel always has a lot of money to show off with at the speedway. He doesn't earn it from a part-time job; he sells stolen bikes to the ring leader at a profit!*

The abandoned shack at Canova Beach is called haunted by the local teens who like to linger on the beach nearby, waiting to see what will happen there. Some say that they have seen a woman who wears an old-fashioned dress wearing boots floating in and out of the walls of the house. Others say that they have seen an Amish-dressed man standing outside the front.

Jane has heard the stories; some have been written about in *Hometown News.* As she waits in her special spot up in the dunes amid the sea grapes later that night, she is able to see up and down the whole length of the shoreline, in which is embedded coquina rocks, large and small.

I've been coming to this special hiding place since I was a little kid, and no one except Mom knows about it.

She listens to the waves breaking on the shore. All at once, she sees a car pull up and park. Four people are inside. Then another car pulls up with two more people. The first car's doors open and out steps Selah, David, Wes, and Daniel. From the other car emerge two girls she recognizes from school, Liz and Toni.

They make no noise, nothing that Jane can hear anyway because of the sound of the waves. They make their way to the front of the old shack. Jane decides she must come out of her hiding place in order to see how they enter the abandoned house, because the door is nailed shut. Daniel pulls back the branches of a large plant near the front door, and Jane watches as the others bend and crawl inside. She notices that there is a small amount of light emanating from what must be a hole in the structure's wall near the ground. *Mr. Potiphar must be inside already*, she thinks to herself.

As soon as Daniel enters and pulls the branches back into place, Jane makes her way to the shack. Quietly she approaches and notices a light shining from a small hole about four inches in diameter, in the plywood, covering one of the windows on the side of the house. It is at the right height for Jane to peer inside.

She sees them sitting at a round table with eight chairs in the center of the small building. There are no inside walls left standing. Jane is looking at one room with a sand-covered floor. A hurricane lantern is flickering in the center of the circular table.

Mr. Potiphar lights a handful of long, narrow sticks of what could be incense, Jane surmises. He blows on them and then places the sticks in a vase on a small table on the opposite side of the house from where Jane stands outside.

The warm sea breeze blows Jane's short brown hair. As the smoke from the incense begins to rise in the air, she hears them begin to chant: "We make a sacred space, a sphere of energy around us filled with moonlight and secrets. The world in our space is beyond time where we converge to cast our spells."

Then Mr. Potiphar speaks: "Tonight, Master of Sorcery, we invite you to bring about your power to cast the spell of…"

Just then a large wave crashes onshore and Jane doesn't hear anything for a moment. She says to herself in a whisper, *what is going on here? A séance or something? If they're casting spells, it must be some sort of witchcraft or sorcery like in* Harry Potter. *How awesome!*

After a few minutes of spying on the secret coven of wizards and witches, Jane's curiosity is satisfied. She wishes she could join them in this fascinating world of theirs, *But I don't have any special abilities. I'm not special in any way.*

CHAPTER 7

Faith is happy that Esther agrees to have lunch with her the next day.

"I'm so pleased to spend this afternoon lunch break from work with you, Essie. It's been too long, and we live right next door to each other!" says Faith, as though that were not an excuse for their neglect of each other.

Esther smiles slightly and takes a forkful of salad.

Faith thinks to herself, *Essie is so much quieter than she was in college. Of course, we're twenty years older now, but she hasn't seemed happy the last few years.*

"Essie, we've always been straight with each other and comfortable talking about anything. I appreciated your friendship in college but, when I was that young, I didn't realize back then how important you were to me. Now that we're older," Faith says with a faint smile, "well, I just wanted you to know that."

Esther replies with, "Isn't it funny how things have turned out? Not the way we had envisioned our futures back then, huh?"

Faith takes a moment to reflect. "Life happens along the way, Essie. The best-laid plans can go astray, or, however that saying goes," she says with a gesture of her hand as if to swish away a fly. "But, if life gives you lemons, then make lemonade!"

Esther can't help but smile with affection for her dear friend who has always had her head in the clouds and thinks that anything can be fixed.

"But!" Esther emphasizes with her index finger in the air. "What if Murphy's Law takes effect, as it often does? Then how do you fix *that*?"

Faith looks perplexed.

"You know, whatever can go wrong, <u>will</u> go wrong."

"I haven't heard that expression in a long time," Faith replies.

Esther shakes her head slightly as she stares at her salad.

Then, looking Faith directly in the eye, Esther confronts her with, "You must have a lot of stress on your job, solving other people's problems all day. How do you stay in a good mood all the time as a social worker? Don't you ever get depressed with all of the people you see every day, not to mention Stephen's death? David and Stephen were very close. Poor boy, losing a friend and his parents; he's always so morose. You're always happy though. What's your secret?"

Inside her mind, Faith is ecstatic at the opening her friend has given her to share her secret; such good news that it's going to blow her friend away.

Faith smiles warmly. *Esther thinks that my serene smile means my secret is going to stay with me.*

Esther continues with anticipation in her voice. "I mean…You have a perfect marriage with Paul…Hey, I haven't seen him for a while. Where's he been?" Without giving Faith a chance to answer, she adds, "And Jane is perfect. She never gives you a hard time talking back to you, like Selah does with me. Jane is a better big sister to Josie than Selah is." Her voice trails off and she lowers her head for another bite of salad.

"Why do you think Selah is disrespectful to you, Essie? Do the two of you ever go out and spend time with each other? Do you ask her what her dreams and desires are?"

Esther raises her eyebrows in surprise as she gapes at her friend across the small table. "We're alone when we go to Orlando," Esther confirms, "and we go shopping together quite often for costumes and dresses for talent shows and movie auditions. In fact, I'm taking her back to Orlando again this Saturday for a second audition for a part in a movie she's perfect for. I'm so excited for her!"

Faith knows what Esther's dreams had been after college. *I think she's projecting her desires onto Selah.* "Is Selah excited, too?" inquires Faith.

Esther purses her lips to think about it before she responds. "I think so. How can she *not* be excited?"

"What sort of activities is she interested in during her spare time? Have you asked her what she wants to study after high school, or where she wants to go to college?"

"She reads a lot of those books about Harry something, goes shopping at the mall with friends and to the speedway on Saturday nights. Oh, and she loves to sing."

"Jane loves to sing, too. She's been in the choir at church and school for a few years now. She reads those books about the 'nice vampires.' Adam reads *Harry Potter*."

"Well, you know that Selah has won many beauty pageants and talent shows with her beautiful voice," Esther replied.

"I know. That's wonderful. Have you asked her how far she would like to take these opportunities she's been fortunate enough to have?"

"What do you mean?"

"I mean, maybe you could start a conversation by asking her if she's really interested in these auditions. Does *she* want to pursue this dream?" Faith notices the confused look as it slowly comes to Esther's face, so she continues by adding, "You know how teenagers can be. Just remember back when we were that age. Dressing Gothic was all the rage at the time, with black lipstick, YUCK! What were we thinking?"

Esther smiles and shakes her head as she remembers. "Yeah; and wearing all black clothes, even dying our hair the blackest we could get it." Esther is amazed at Faith's use of the old fashioned word "rage" as the term to identify what everyone was doing as a fad so long ago. "All we wanted to do was to listen to *The Grateful Dead* rock band and show off our outrageous ways of dressing so we could freak out the older generation. The more tattoos and piercings, the better!" They both laugh in a moment of shared camaraderie.

"Let's see," says Faith when she stops laughing. "What's all the rage now? Reading those *Harry Potter* books and practicing sorcery as wizards and witches; those books about the 'gorgeous vampires' who only hunt animals and sparkle in the sunlight." Faith seems to pull herself off this train of thought, then continues, "Seriously though, Essie, you should find out what Selah has in mind for her future. If she's lost interest in these auditions you make her go to, then she *is* going to rebel and take it out on you. Her disrespect for you will only increase if you make her do something she doesn't want to do." Faith waits and wonders how her friend will respond to this insight that has suddenly been revealed.

Esther leans back in her chair like someone who has just received shocking news. "I think her boyfriend, Wes, is more important to her right now. She's got her priorities mixed up for the time being, that's all. I'll make her understand what's important. I'm sure that she will thank me later when she's discovered by a talent agency. In fact, I can be her talent agent; keep the money in the family, right?"

"Essie, you really need to consider that maybe you're projecting your desires onto your daughter. In my opinion, and from all that I've read on the subject, experts agree that parents should ask their teens about _their_ hopes and dreams for _their_ future. When you do, chances are that Selah will be honest with you. Give her more freedom of choice and she'll develop more responsibility for the consequences of her own decisions. Have a positive attitude when she opens up and tells you what she wants."

Esther sits unmoving for what seems like a long, awkward moment, but Faith gives her friend time to absorb all that she has heard. _Is she contemplating what I've said, or is she about to cry?_ wonders Faith with trepidation in her heart.

To break the unnerving silence, Faith speaks tenderly. "Well, think about what we've discussed. In the meantime, you had asked me about my secret for dealing with stress, anxiety, and depression…. Here's my answer: I received my peace and happiness about a year ago by studying and following the teachings of the most unique and exceptional man who ever lived."

Esther stares at her friend with both hope and fear in her eyes as Faith reaches in her purse and then pushes a small booklet across the table toward her.

"Jesus."

Esther sighs deeply and drops her head in disbelief. "What? Oh, c'mon, Faith, that's ridiculous. Don't tell me that you've been brainwashed by some religious cult! The Bible is full of contradictions and a bunch of things that don't make any sense at all. I don't know why I keep going to church; it's just a waste of time."

"Why _do_ you go to church then, Esther? Don't you believe that there really is a God? Somewhere deep inside you want to believe. We all are interested in the supernatural. God made us that way so we would search for Him; and when you find Him, you will never be the same again."

CHAPTER 8

On Saturday, as Selah and Esther are on their way back from Orlando, there is complete silence in the car for the hour's drive. Selah had blown her chance at getting the small part in the new movie being made. Now she must wait for the next opportunity.

Esther was confused. *Selah has always been excited about the possibility of acting and modeling. What's changed? I don't understand.*

Jane and Josie have taken the notebook over to Josie's room, while Selah and Esther are on their way back from Orlando.

"Won't it be awesome if Selah gets discovered?" asks Josie. "My beautiful sister in a movie! Are you ready now? You OK?" she questions as she lay the notebook on her lap. They both sit cross-legged on Josie's bed.

"Sure. Let me read it to you this time, all right?"

Josie lingers with a cherubic smile and hands the notebook to Jane.

"From: **BibleStudyPlanet.com**; 'Evidence that God Exists; Three Basic Proofs.' (Paraphrased):

1. The Evidence of Cause.

    a) The universe had a beginning. Anything that has a beginning must have been caused by something else.

b) That 'something else' was God. To give an example, this paper did not write itself. Something else caused it to appear (that something else was me).

2. The Evidence of Design.

a) Design implies a designer.

b) The universe and humans are an intricately complicated design.

c) There is a Great Designer who made the universe and humans. Example: If you find a computer lying out in a field, would you say that it evolved, or that it was created? A computer is too complex to exist without someone building it. We are far more complex and advanced than a computer. DNA, in every cell of the human body, can store three times as much information as thirty volumes of The Encyclopedia Britannica. Such a complex design of codes could only have been created by an intelligence and not by evolutionary happenstance.

3. The Evidence of Moral Law.

a) Every human is aware that there is a moral standard.

b) Moral laws imply a Moral Lawgiver.

c) So logic says that there must be a Supreme Moral Lawgiver.

From the website of **www.ItIsWritten.org**:

"The design of the human body demands the existence of a designer. Have you ever pondered…everything that is involved in the simple act of seeing? The delicate engineering of the eye… make[s] the most advanced camera seem like a simple child's toy in comparison, and no computer can even come close to duplicating the intricate workings of the eye.

"If you believe in evolution instead of creation, the minute details involved in eyesight would be impossible to develop by natural selection…. Darwin himself admitted that vision had to have been designed all at once because of all the systems depending on each other for incredibly complicated tasks. The entire human body is made that way—each organ depending on another for proper functioning of the whole.

"Some thoughts for you to ponder:

1. How likely is it that if you wrote the numbers from 1 through 10 on different slips of paper (one number to a sheet of paper), put them into an opaque container and then pull them out in numerical order? The law of mathematics says you would have only one chance in 10,000,000,000 (ten billion)! Would evolution by natural selection fit this equation, or would a superior intelligence be more likely to create that chance?

2. What are the chances that a chimpanzee, even if given lessons, could write a book as detailed as *War and Peace*?

3. Dr. Arthur Conklin wrote: 'The probability of life originating from an accident is comparable to the probability of an unabridged dictionary resulting from an explosion in a print shop.'

4. If life was not intelligently created by a superior being, then one would probably believe that if letters from a Scrabble game were thrown into the air that they would land to form a complete, correctly structured sentence. Not very likely, huh, even after a million throws trying to get that result.

"If you don't believe that God exists, then do you believe that the above examples of evolution's theory are more likely to be true?"

As soon as Esther pulls into the driveway, Selah jumps out of the car without waiting for the garage door to fully open and races into her room, slamming the door behind her.

Esther wants so badly to console her daughter, but thinks it best not to bother her right now. *Let her calm down from her humiliating audition and we can talk later.*

In her room, Selah is nauseous. The piercing anxiety in her pounding heart and in her abdomen has dwindled somewhat, but it's still too much for her to bear. She has books of information from Mr. Potiphar at the top of her closet, where she keeps them hidden from her mother. *I have to find that spell that creates serenity in my being and the one for control over others.* She consults the index of her files. "Ah, the Book of Sorcery and Shadows! This is what I need!"

Josie hears her mother and sister come in, but she is not worried. The door to her room is closed. Jane hears Selah and Esther now also. The two girls look at each other. Suddenly, there is a knock on the door. "Josie," Esther intrudes as she opens the door.

Jane calmly closes the notebook and leaves it on her lap. Josie looks to Jane with apprehension in her eyes, but Jane gives a reassuring smile.

"Hello, Mrs. A."

"Hi, Jane. Any problems?"

"No, never. How's everything with you?"

"Don't ask. I need some time with Selah alone. Would you mind taking Josie over to your house so you can finish reading the story to her?"

Esther waits until Jane and Josie close the front door to the house.

After only a few minutes with Selah, Esther screams, "What do you mean, you're giving up cheerleading?" Esther is in shock as she stands in Selah's bedroom.

"Exactly what I said. I don't want to be a cheerleader next year. From now on, I'm going to do what *I* want to do!"

Esther stands silently, dumbstruck at what she has heard from her daughter. She gazes at Selah's stern and determined stance, with her arms folded across her chest in defiance.

Esther thinks, *maybe I am being too demanding, just as Faith had said. I can't push my desires onto Selah.* Esther slowly sits down in the chair at Selah's desk. *Faith warned me that Selah would become more rebellious if I become too pushy.*

Selah's sudden assertive tone of voice jolts Esther out of her heart-pounding thoughts. "Now, if you don't mind, I have plans tonight." Selah walks to the bedroom door and holds it open with her hand on the knob while she taps her foot with disrespect and impatience.

After pausing long enough to clear her head, Esther chokes back tears and attempts to respond with a positive attitude. "OK. That's fine. I'm proud of you for making a decision and following through with it. Maybe you feel that it's time for you to grow up and try your own ways." Esther stands and smiles lightly with hurt in her eyes at her contemptuous daughter. She realizes at this moment how much Selah reminds her of herself at age sixteen. *It hurts to discover how stubborn and prideful we both are.*

Selah is absolutely thunderstruck as her mother walks slowly to where she stands, but continues berating her mother with an air of authority. "And furthermore, *I* say when we go to Orlando."

Esther sighs deeply and reluctantly submits. "You're right. If your heart's not in it, it will simply be a waste of time. I'm sorry; I shouldn't have been so pushy and demanding toward you. I sincerely thought I was doing what was best for you." The utter sadness in Esther's eyes goes unnoticed by Selah as her mother slowly turns and walks out the door.

With a puzzled look on her face, Selah closes the door. All at once, her mouth falls open in amazement and she raises her hands over her head in victory. "YES! Thank you, Goddess of Shadows, for your book of spells!"

CHAPTER 9

Rocky Water Mall is filled the following Saturday with people looking to escape the July afternoon heat. Daniel receives his hamburger as he sees Jane round the corner of the California Cookie Company, walking in his direction. Selah orders Chinese food.

"There she is, Selah." Daniel stays standing to draw Jane's attention. He and Selah both smile and wave Jane over to their table through the crowd.

Jane takes a deep breath with some anxiety over being invited to lunch completely out of the blue by kids with whom she has never before socialized. She was awake most of last night twitching with nervous excitement and curiosity.

Now, as Jane walks toward them, she wonders, *why all of a sudden do they want to acknowledge that I exist?*

Daniel pulls out the chair to his left across the table from Selah.

"I bought you a hamburger with lots of pickles, just like Josie told me that you liked, and a raspberry iced tea. I hope you don't mind. Josie talks a lot about you."

Jane sits down next to Daniel, a slight smile on her face. "Thank you, Daniel," she says as she eyes him with cautious curiosity. Then she looks over at Selah. "Why did you call and ask me to meet you here today?"

Selah smiles, looks down at her cup and moves her straw up and down through the hole in the lid, making a squonking sound. "Josie talks so much about you that I thought maybe we could hang out together. After all, you and I have known each other since sixth grade."

Daniel adds with a charming smile, "Yeah, Selah, David and I have talked about it and we'd like to get to know you better." After some hesitation, he adds, "There is another reason why we have asked you here, Jane. We need your expert help."

"You want my help? With what?" Jane is thunderstruck.

Daniel replies, "A group of us gets together at Dragon Point inside Annie and we have lots of fun. Well, you'll see, if you want to join us. We need a secretary to take notes at our meetings. Do you think you might like to join us as part of our group? We sure could use your expert note-taking abilities at our meetings."

Jane looks over at Selah who adds, "Yeah, we've had classes together all of these years, Jane, and it would be nice to have you in our group and get to know you."

Noticing that she has been holding her breath, Jane slowly exhales, leans forward to place her elbow on the table, and begins to rub her forehead in disbelief. She listens to the din of voices in the large open area. Sunlight streams through the overhead skylights. The ringing in her ears blends with the loud murmurs of the surrounding people and, to Jane, it sounds like the roaring of many lions hungering for prey. The cacophony reverberates back and forth in her head until she becomes aware of the weight on her chest. She can hardly believe this is happening. *How can I say no? They want me to hang with them!* She makes her decision. "Of course, I'll be glad to help you by taking the minutes of your meetings. What kind of meetings do you have at Dragon Point?"

"You'll see," responds Selah.

In the meantime, David is in the mall with two members of the gang. Liz and Toni, his companions at the beach house séance, walk away arm-in-arm from the three boys. David's face burns with fiery embarrassment, and he finds it difficult to hide the embers of humiliation that churn to the surface like heaving lumps of hot lava.

He stares with incredulity as Liz departs after rejecting his invitation of a date with him. *I was positive that she would go out with me. Hasn't she been flirting with me at every séance in the haunted house and in classes at school? I didn't know that she only likes girls!* David's hands are clenched fists that resemble the spiked balls used by ancient Roman gladiators. His temples throb and he wants to run away. *No! I won't run! I'm not a coward!*

Instead, David turns around to face the two other boys with him at the mall. He attempts to slough off his humiliating rejection. "Aaahhh! You know how some girls are. It's hard to tell what's really going on in their minds, but we have to try, right? And, you know what else? If she had said yes, I would have told her that I was standing in for you, Bruce, because you would have wet your pants if you had tried to ask her out!"

Jeers and laughter erupt from the boys and Wes begins playfully knocking Bruce around. David feels less embarrassed now that he's embarrassed Bruce. He becomes emboldened and finally acknowledges Adam Wilson and Jared Preston, who always follow his group around the mall. Both younger boys have their hands in their pockets and feign window shopping when they notice David glancing their way.

"Hey, Wes and Bruce! Do you wanna have some fun and put these two guys to the test? Let's see how badly they want to join our gang."

Wes is surprised at David's sudden assertiveness without Daniel's presence. "They don't belong with us. They're wimps; they won't pass the test."

David responds with arrogance, "What do *you* know? When they <u>do</u> pass our initiation test, we'll swear them to secrecy and they can be our errand boys. They'll love it!" His reply is meant to humiliate Wes.

"Hey! You two!" David yells to the boys who are about ten yards away. "Come here," he demands as he gestures for them to approach.

Adam and Jared look astonished as they stare at each other with their mouths agape. They turn to David and, with inquisitive looks on their faces, each points to his own chest.

"Yeah! You two, Adam and Jared; get over here."

As the two boys walk shyly toward the group, Wes says, "That's Jane Wilson's and Donna Preston's little brothers, right? They're junior high punks, Dave. Leave them alone. We don't want *kids* hangin' around with us."

David ignores Wes's remark. "Run when I call you!" he bellows through clenched teeth to the two boys.

Adam and Jared, already full of trepid expectancy, pick up their pace to a jog until they reach the older boys.

In a toned down way so as to not draw attention from the crowd walking by, David orders, "Stand at attention!"

The two boys do as they are ordered, but both are noticeably nervous.

David begins to pace slowly back and forth with his hands clasped behind his back like a drill sergeant. "So, you two think that you're brave enough to be part of our gang?"

Wes pulls David away from earshot of the younger boys. "Dave, do you think that this is something Dan would approve of?"

David looks numbly at Wes. He simply turns away from him and continues in the manner of a drill sergeant with Adam and Jared. "Well, do you think that you have what it takes to join us?"

They both nod their heads. David wants to order them to say, "Yes, sir," but thinks better of it under the circumstances.

"I assume you both know what the initiation test consists of. Do you have the guts for it?"

They look at each other and again nod in the positive to David's question, but Adam detects fear in Jared's eyes. *Is he going to wimp out on me? We're finally going to get what we have been wanting; what we've talked about all year long.* It is now that Adam realizes that only he has talked about wanting to be part of the gang. Jared has never expressed his thoughts on the matter.

David stops pacing and looks directly at Adam and Jared, while Bruce and Wes stand back a short distance watching the scene unfold. "Here are the rules," begins David. "You must steal something from the cutlery store or tobacco shop; something small enough to fit into your pocket, and that can't be detected electronically as you leave with the item of your choice. It will then be kept in our hideout as a trophy to your bravery and your ability to stay calm under stress. You'll each be observed by one of these guys," he says as he points over his shoulder to Wes and Bruce, "who'll be an eyewitness to the theft.

"You and your witness will enter the store separately; you will wait until he is in the same aisle, so he can observe your act. After retrieving the object, which is now in your pants pocket, you must use your own cunning to complete the test and escape undetected. If you get caught, Wes or Bruce, whoever I appoint as your witness, will then cover for you by telling the employee that you are his little brother and that he intended to pay for it.

"You will then proceed immediately to the nearest exit, where you will show us the item. Is that understood?"

Adam nods with wide open eyes, obviously nervous. Jared stares down at the floor at an invisible stone in his mind, which has engraved on it the words of the Eighth Commandment: "Thou shalt not steal."

David lowers his head to the level of Jared's, which is still turned downward. With a pause in between his words to add emphasis, "Is... that...understood...soldier?"

Jared swallows deeply with fear. By this time, Adam turns to look at his friend in bewilderment as David spits out his next words through clenched teeth.

"Cat got your tongue, little girl?"

Jared again swallows hard and deep. "I will not steal, nor do I want to be associated with thieves. You don't intimidate me, you low-life bullies." He raises his chin in defiance. He is scared out of his wits as his gaze meets David's.

Adam's mouth falls open in disbelief at what he has just heard. No one has ever dared to stand up to one of these gang members before.

Jared isn't sure what to do next. He turns to Adam, expecting him to stand up against this giant bully also.

David is caught unexpectedly in another humiliating situation in front of the other gang members. He takes a step backward and changes the amazed look he knows is on his face to a squinting glare which he directs at Jared. David takes a deep breath, flares his nostrils and puffs up his chest. "OK, little girl, you scared baby. Run to your mommy with your tail between your legs. GO!" David demands as he points back in the direction from which Jared had come. With his glare still fixed on Jared's eyes, he adds, "I don't want cowards in my platoon!"

Jared's heart races wildly. He wants Adam to turn around and walk away from this situation too, but he can't seem to move. He will not leave his friend. After what seems to Jared like an hour, he turns away from David's menacing scowl and looks at Adam, who stares at him with a confused expression.

"Adam?" Jared squeaks with imploring eyes, but Adam's mind is not on his friend. It's on his sister; he knows that she wants to be accepted by this clique of popular kids. *If I can be accepted by David and Daniel, then maybe they would accept Jane into their group, too.*

David interrupts Adam's faulty deductive reasoning. "Are you gonna crawl away on your belly like this bawling baby, huh? Are you a spineless Jesus freak like him?"

Adam's eyes are still fixed on Jared.

With narrowed eyes, David growls, "Adam! Look at me!"

All of a sudden, Adam recalls the talk his mother had had with him. Her face had been sad and her eyes moist. As he lay on his bed one night, mad at her, she had asked, "Adam, how could you thank someone who took your place on death row for something *you* had done against the law?" Adam was taken aback and was tongue-tied. He simply stared at her with a stupefied glaze in his eyes. She had continued with an even more bizarre question. "If you didn't know that he had willingly taken your place until after he had already died, how could you thank him for saving your life and taking the penalty for you?"

"I don't know, Mom; by turning myself in to the police and confessing?"

"Exactly. By admitting that *you* are the one who is guilty of the sin, not this other man who died in your place; that you want to say how sorry you are for breaking the law and that you will be a completely different person, worthy of the sacrifice that this man has made for you. He died so that you could live."

Adam had cocked his head deep in thought and replied, "Sort of like in the movie, *Saving Private Ryan,* when, at the end, the man who was dying said, 'Be worthy of this.'?"

His mother had simply smiled and nodded her head. Then she had explained how a man such as this could be repaid for the selfless sacrifice that he had made for *him*.

With a sorrowful look at Jared, Adam turns his heavy heart to face David, ignoring the words his mother had told him. "I'm not a coward. I can pass your stupid test." There, he's done it. Adam realizes that he has inadvertently called his friend a coward. But it is too late; the words have been spoken and he can't take them back. Adam is too scared to follow Jared's exemplary lead. Out of the corner of his eye, Adam notices his best friend's shoulders slump and his head drop in despair. He hears Jared's disappointed sigh. Adam is unable to look at him. As Jared slowly turns and walks away, Adam is unaware of the tears in his best friend's eyes.

CHAPTER 10

"Adam! Are you crazy?" asks Jane the next morning. "What if you had gotten caught?"

"No problem. They had 'Plan B' figured out. Now we're both part of the coolest gang at school where I'll be a sophomore in the fall!"

"My situation was different, though, Adam. They asked for my note-taking skills. Have you ever stolen anything before yesterday?"

"No, but it was a rush!"

"Yeah? Well, Jared was the smarter one. Do you know that you have broken one of God's Ten Commandments?" Jane replies.

"Oh, so what? It's not like I killed someone, you know. Geez! Soldiers kill in war.

"And where's God anyway? If He really exists, why do all these bad things happen in the world? Huh? Like what happened to Stephen? Answer that one, 'Miss High and Mighty Know-it-All!' I wish I could get a gun and blow away that murderer just like he did to Stephen! Also, why do you think that Dad left? He doesn't want a religious fanatic for a wife, that's why. Mom has gone insane with her 'Jesus Freak' ways."

"Dad said he was away on business the last time he called," retorts Jane.

"Duh, hello. Don't you know what's really going on?"

Jane is quiet for a moment and leans back on her bed with a sigh of confusion. *Yeah, I know. I just don't want it to be true. Dad's been gone for almost a year now.*

Adam interrupts her thoughts. "Maybe they finally noticed that we're cool."

Jane sits up and concentrates on her new status as a soon-to-be senior. "Maybe you're right, Adam. Isn't it great? We get to hang out with the cool kids this summer at Dragon Point!"

They hear their mother's voice. "C'mon kids, I don't want to be late to church."

"We're coming, Mom," Jane responds. "Adam, promise me that you won't do anything to get into *big* trouble. If Mom knew what you did…" Jane shakes her head.

"OK. I won't steal anymore. I know it was wrong, but it was like I was being tempted or dared or something. I had to do it, can't you see that? It was a matter of pride."

"I hope that we don't regret this decision to hang around with bike thieves."

"Bike thieves?" Adam is confused.

"I'll tell you later."

It is difficult for Adam to sit in church. He doesn't want to be here. He feels no guilt about what he did to Jared, but he feels proud to be accepted by the popular kids at school, and he contemplates his new status for the coming school year. He looks over at David with the Abrams, and Daniel with his father, sitting in the pews like good little saints. *David and Daniel steal bikes; Daniel and his father both curse enough to embarrass a Marine. Hypocrites!*

After the service, Selah walks over to invite Jane and Adam to their first meeting at Dragon Point. "Let's get changed and meet there in two hours. Don't forget your steno pad and pencil, Miss Secretary! See ya there."

Adam stares as usual at the beauty of Selah Rose Abrams. *I've never seen anyone more beautiful, even in magazines.*

Reading her brother's expression, Jane warns, "Don't even think about it, Adam. She's off limits, you hear me?"

"Of course, *big* sister," he responds with sarcasm about her height.

With smiles of affection for each other and anticipation of the meeting, Adam and Jane walk to the car to have lunch with their mother at their favorite diner, as is their custom.

Faith speaks briefly with Esther and John. "If we don't have different plans, we should ride together to church from now on to save gas." After a moment's pause, Faith asks, "Would you all like to join us for lunch at Harold's Diner?"

John answers, "Yes, that would be nice, don't you think, Esther?"

Esther shrugs her shoulders and quietly submits to the invitation.

After everyone orders, David sits deep in thought. *I really don't see any point in attending church. The place is full of self-righteous hypocrites. They go to church every Sunday, and then live like crude animals the rest of the week. What's the point in listening to boring sermons? Who cares about what happened to a man two thousand years ago? What's that got to do with me? We live and then we die. That's it, there is no God. Stephen was my best friend and now he's gone.*

David looks over at Adam, who is already looking his way. He thinks, *Daniel and I didn't make a mistake in recruiting Adam into our group did we?. Wes doesn't know that Dan and I had it all planned out that day at the mall.*

Jane sits on the outside of the large booth and Josie is next to the wall on the opposite side of the table. *This is the first time that all of us have had a meal together,* Jane thinks. *Selah has always made me feel inferior to her; but look at us now. We're eating at the same table, right across from each other!*

Josie surveys the table full of the people she loves most. *Except Stephen's not here; I wonder where he went. Where is he now? What happens after we die?*

Josie notices a wall-mounted television near the ceiling. One of the news stations is reporting from the Middle East, describing the killing of Christians by ISIS. She interrupts the quiet niceties being nervously spoken around her at the table. "Why?" she asks to no one in particular. "Why do we kill each other when we're all going to die anyway?"

The other seven at the table become still. Deep down inside, they are grateful that Josie has begun a conversation. Esther hasn't spoken to Faith since their lunch together two weeks ago.

John answers, "Well, they attacked our country, honey, and our President told our soldiers and marines that their special knowledge and skills were needed over there to keep the bad people from attacking anyone else, or us, again."

"I don't think that we should treat each other like that," Josie responds. "Isn't it the same thing when someone is mean to me? Should I treat him the same way? Mrs. Wilson told me that we should not…what was the word you used?" She looks directly at Faith with sensitive eyes.

"You mean, *retaliate*?" Faith supplied.

"Yeah! That's the word; and there's another word for when we see things in a different way." Again she looks to Faith for the answer.

"Um, let's see. 'Point of View'?"

Josie's face brightens as she continues, with her thoughts being expressed aloud.

"Everyone has a point of view except God. He has points to view."[1]

Now everyone regards Faith as the one to deal with this conversation. All but Faith and Jane are timid and fretful.

Faith replies, "Maybe a better way to say it would be *viewing points*. Is that what you mean?"

"Yeah, so even though we are like Him, He is different from us."

David is quiet for a moment, then his face lights up with an idea that has taken shape in his mind also.

"OK, I see. People have an infinite amount of points of view, but God has an infinite amount of viewing points."[2]

"YES! That can only mean," adds Josie, "that God is everywhere at the same time! But God is different from us in another way; He can know everybody's inside thoughts, but we can only know them from the outside. When Stephen told me that he thought there was a fourth dimension for people to find, I think that it is inside me, because God knows what's on the inside of everybody. God must be in the fourth dimension!"[3] Her eyes are alight with exuberant revelation. Then she becomes sullen before asking, "But why isn't He on the inside of everyone, so there would be no bad people? Is anybody good enough to find the fourth dimension, and to go to heaven?"

"Jesus was the only one of us who was," answers Jane as she watches Josie absorb this deep conversation.

Suddenly, Jane is embarrassed in front of everyone because Faith and Josie are the only ones who don't turn their gaze away from her. Instead, her mother gives her a smile and puts her arm around her.

David and Selah look at each other with the same thought: *Oh no! She isn't going to start preaching to us now, is she? Did we make a mistake inviting her to hang with us?*

Adam looks across the table at David, with a roll of his eyes and a shake of his head, to let David know that he doesn't go along with all this gibberish.

Again, Josie fills the silence and changes the subject. "Hey, do you all know that room spelled backwards is moor? A room is a space with walls and what's a moor, Daddy?"

"A moor is a wide open space that has no walls."

"So then they're antonyms, opposites, like light and dark. Lived spelled backwards is devil," she says before she tucks a french fry in her mouth. "So that must mean that they're opposites, too. Do ya get it?"

Josie looks around at everyone whose mouths are agape at her train of thought. She sighs with exasperation and crosses her arms. "It means that we live opposite from the devil. We are like God who is the light and the devil is the darkness. Satan is mean and we should be the opposite of the devil. What was his name that God gave him?"

Faith gives the answer, "Lucifer, who can trick us and appear as an angel of light." Faith treads carefully here. She is being led to take Josie's train of thought a bit deeper. "But didn't Jesus say, 'I am the Light'?" Faith inquires. "Why did He say it *like that*?" [3]

Josie thinks hard for a moment. "So we won't get confused?"

Faith watches Josie's eyes sparkle with intensity as the information sinks in further.

"OH! There are two lights: One is God and the 'pretend' one is Satan. The devil tricks people because he is the opposite kind of light from God. The real light is Jesus!" Josie is ecstatic, Faith is thrilled, and the others stare at each other with confusion and disgust at this conversation by 'Jesus freaks'. Josie simply shrugs her shoulders and smashes a french fry into the smear of ketchup on her plate.

"Is everyone ready to go? We all have plans together," says Selah, with hasty impatience in her tone of voice, in order to stop the ridiculous nonsense that she is hearing.

Faith directs a question to Selah. "So, Selah what *are* your plans for today? Are you all going to the beach?"

"We don't know yet. We just want to hang out, right guys?" she inquires as she looks at Jane.

"Yeah, Mom," clarifies Jane. "We're just going to hang out together for a while, if that's OK."

"It's OK with me. Shall we go then?" Faith responds.

CHAPTER 11

Thirty minutes later, Jane and Adam sit next to each other inside Annie's belly, anxiously awaiting what the afternoon will bring.

Selah is still outside talking with Wes, while David and Daniel get things set up for the session.

"Hey, c'mon you guys; we're ready for you to join us," says Daniel to Wes and Selah as he sits cross-legged on the floor. "Jane, I want you and Adam to sit out of the circle for our first attempt at contacting the spirits, so PAY ATTENTION!"

They both move to the side and allow Selah and Wes to join the circle.

"Is Bruce coming today?" Wes asks Daniel.

At the mention of his name, Bruce joins the group. "The more the merrier is what I say. What do you say, Wes?"

"Hey! Glad you're here, buddy!" Wes responds with enthusiasm.

Jane opens her note pad and notices that Selah is not as happy to see Bruce as Wes seems to be.

Daniel looks to Jane. "Pay close attention and do as we talked about, OK? Write down the letters as they are spelled out on the board with the planchette. No talking, either one of you. I have to see if the spirits will even show up with you two here." Then with a lighthearted smile he adds, "Maybe they won't even like you."

Brother and sister watch as the others, all sitting cross-legged on the floor, straighten their backs, close their eyes and begin to hum softly. This goes on for about two minutes.

"We invite you to join us today," Daniel speaks softly and slowly. "Come, spirits of the darkness. Answer our questions."

They all touch the planchette lightly and begin to hum again.

Daniel questions slowly, "What is your name?"

M-O-L-E-C-H

"Where are you from?"

A-N-C-I-E-N-T-U-N-I-V-E-R-S-E

"How did you die?"

D-I-D-N-O-T-D-I-E-N-E-V-E-R-D-I-E-C-H-I-L-D-R-E-N-S-A-C-R-I-F-I-C-E-D

They all look at each other with confusion in their attempt to understand what has just been spelled out to them. Suddenly, they hear a slow, sardonic chuckle. At this, they pull back their hands from the planchette in a state of fear, all except Daniel.

Selah gasps. David is scared also but says, "Whoa! That's never happened before!"

Jane and Adam sit in a state of shock momentarily, their eyes wide with fright. Finally, Jane finds her voice. "What just happened here?"

Daniel shrieks with trepid excitement, "HA HA! We've got it now! That was so awesome, it's almost unbelievable! Everybody heard that, right?"

Everyone nods their head as if in a state of shock.

"Rats! We lost the spirit when we broke contact with the Ouija board," Daniel scolds.

"Maybe not, let's keep going," David expresses hopefully. "See, Wes. They brought more power to the circle. They're not wimps," David says happily while looking at Jane and Adam. Wes simply blushes with embarrassment at the words he had spoken in confidence that day at the mall.

Adam looks at Wes with an arrogant expression as if to say, *I told you so.*

With some hesitation, David reaches out to the planchette, and the others follow his lead.

"Wait!" yells Daniel. He begins a slow, caustic smile before he says, "We can hold a séance to see if we can get Molech to speak to us, and maybe even make an appearance!" His eyes are bright with excitement.

"I don't think we should," warns Selah. "Mr. Potiphar says we are not ready to do a séance without him present. We're not experienced enough." Selah stands up and walks to the door. "I'm outta here."

She stops and turns around to look at her friends. "That scared the wits outta me, and the rest of you look scared to death, too. Admit it."

Jane decides to stand up and leave with Selah. "You guys are crazy if you think I'm gonna stay and let some demonic ghost take possession of our minds or something."

David is in turmoil. He is trembling from fright and wants to leave also, but his pride won't let him. "We just contacted the supernatural world! How can we leave now?"

Jane stares at her brother and immediately knows that he needs some help in order to keep his pride in front of the other boys, but she doesn't know what to do. *I've already stood up to leave with Selah, but I can't leave Adam here.*

"OK," Selah says to give everyone a way out of this without anyone's pride being hurt. "Let's tell Mr. Potiphar about this and see what he says. He told me that we can call him anytime we need him, and boy, do we need him now. Come outside with me and I'll use my cell phone to call him. I need all of you with me to prove to him what happened here today."

Selah opens the door and holds it wide open for all to leave. The boys don't admit to each other that they are trembling inside, and are relieved to be let out of there.

Daniel thinks to himself, *I wonder why I'm letting Selah give the orders all of a sudden.*

"Hello, Mr. Potiphar. This is Selah. I hope I'm not bothering you, but you _did_ say we could call you if we needed to."

"It's perfectly all right. Is everything OK?"

"Well, something unexpected—and a little disturbing—just happened with the Ouija board. We all heard the ghost laughing. That's never happened before. It scared us so much that we broke contact. Should we continue? We need your advice."

"Let me ask you one thing. What was different about your session today, besides the audible occurrence?"

"We invited two new people to join us," Selah answers. She turns to the others and asks, "Was there anything else different that we did today, before or during the session?"

Everyone shakes their heads in agreement that there hadn't been.

"Those two people must have an unusually strong connection to the spirit world in order to bring about such an occurrence. I'd like to meet them. Let's have a special meeting at the beach house tonight at 7:30. Can everyone make it?"

Selah repeats what Mr. Potiphar had asked. "Yeah, we can make it, Mr. P."

Mr. Potiphar adds, "And bring that Ouija board with you."

At 7:50 that night, Selah, David, Daniel, and Wes stand outside of the beach house, waiting until they are called to come inside.

"I'm so curious," Selah says. "What could Mr. Potiphar have to say to Jane and Adam that he doesn't want us to hear?"

Wes tries to dispel her curiosity. "We're supposed to trust him, remember? He knows what he's doing."

Inside, Jane and Adam are curious about this man also. "So, you're brother and sister, huh? I heard about your brother Stephen. I'm sorry. Tell me how you feel about this terrible thing that has happened to you and your parents."

As the older sibling, Jane feels compelled to speak first. "Have you ever had anything like this happen to you, Mr. Potiphar? How do you think *you* would feel?"

"Yes, you're right, Jane, of course. All I meant was that venting your anger to someone can be very helpful in releasing the pent-up hatred and rage you both must be feeling inside for the boy who murdered your brother."

He looks at both of them and asks, "If you are going to be part of this very special group—and you are both very special to have been invited— then I would like to get to know you a little better. I hope that's all right," he says in a sweet, condescending manner.

"Yeah, it's all right Mr. Potiphar," responds Adam. "I'm mad at a lot of things. My mom and dad, the insane idiot who murdered my brother... but most of all how could God—if there is a God—let this happen? Nothing is fair in life, nothing. Not even..." Adam stops and looks at Jane. "Not even the fact that you breeze through school, and Mom and Dad are always on me about my grades. Sometimes I even get mad at *you,* Jane."

Jane glares at her brother. "What do you get mad at me for? I offer to help you with your homework, but your stupid pride gets in the way."

Mr. Potipher is pleased, very pleased indeed. *My ploy has worked to get them **raging mad** and test my theory!* He smiles inside as he listens to them.

"And besides," continues Jane, "Don't you think that I have feelings of anger, too? I hate that boy who shot Stephen and I can't even get back at him because he's *dead!*"

Outside the small shack, Selah could be patient no longer. She walks to the opening near the ground outside the old house and, looking around to make sure that there is no one around to see her, pulls back the plant as she hears Jane's and Adam's voices.

Mr. Potiphar sees her and gestures for her to come inside. The boys enter also and make their way to the table near Adam and Jane, who by this time notice their friends' arrival and quit arguing.

Jane is surprised to see the Ouija board already set up in front of Mr. Potiphar as David, Daniel, Wes, and Selah fill in the chairs around the table. She also sees a look of pleasure on Mr. Potiphar's face.

"It is good that the power of your combined anger has drawn many spirits around us tonight. You both are very special indeed, just as Selah says you are."

When did I say that these two geeks were special? Selah thinks to herself. *Mr. P is losing it, for sure.*

"Come now." Mr. Potiphar begins. "Let us join our power of anger and our minds to the supernatural realm. They are waiting for us. Touch lightly and close your eyes."

After only a few minutes, the planchette begins to move slowly at first, and then starts moving rapidly as everyone opens their eyes to watch. Jane and Adam are not touching the planchette, but Mr. Potiphar insists that they join them.

"Brother and sister, join us. Touch, and communicate with the spirits."

They both look at each other and slowly reach out for the planchette.

"Who is with us tonight?" Mr. Potiphar asks with a strange look of delight on his face. "Powers of darkness, we beckon you to enter our sphere and speak with us."

Suddenly, they are taken aback at the sound of "something" walking across the creaky, sand-covered floor. It's not human. Despite the humid July evening, an icy coldness swirls silently around the table as the sound of footsteps continues across the room. Then, abruptly, the sound ceases. No one moves or makes a sound.

Suddenly, Mr. Potiphar grunts with a spasmodic jerk to his entire body. The group stares with disbelief as their leader is overcome with torpor. His hands fall to his sides and his head drops to his chest. Selah has never seen this happen before, and breaks her connection to the planchette. The others follow her lead and stare at Mr. Potiphar.

Selah reaches out to touch Mr. Potiphar's arm, but Daniel stops her. She looks at Daniel who slowly shakes his head and puts his finger to his mouth for silence as he glares around the table at the others to do the same.

All at once, Mr. Potiphar raises his head with a quick movement. His eyes look like black holes in his head. It seems as if there is nothing behind them. His mouth moves with grotesque distortions, but no sound comes out.

Daniel splits the terror-filled silence. "What is your name?"

The voice that comes out of the mouth of Mr. Potiphar frightens David to his very core. "I AM LEGION."[1]

With horror, David recognizes the rumbling snarl of the spine-chilling words spewing out of this man in front of him. It's the sound in his dreams, the all-too-real nightmares he has, night after night. He jumps up, tipping over his chair. The others at the table stare up at David, who is frozen in place, unable to move.

Suddenly, Mr. Potiphar is once again himself—or is he?

"It's OK. There's nothing to be frightened of," he says. "We have accomplished much this evening thanks to Adam and Jane." He glares at all of them with those vacant, black holes. *Yes,* he thinks to himself. *Anger and hatred are powerful indeed!* "You may leave me now," he suddenly orders them as he continues to stare blankly into the hurricane lamp on the table.

Then they hear the same sardonic chuckle they had heard earlier inside the dragon emanating from the man with the black, vacant eyes.

They hasten to the opening in the wall and crawl out, not taking their eyes off of Mr. Potiphar.

Outside, on the eerie moonlit beach, they all look at each other with amazed excitement.

"Wasn't that awesome?" exclaims Daniel. "I've never experienced anything like that before!"

"That was wild!" adds Selah.

Daniel inquires, "Did everyone feel that cold chill in the room?"

Jane and Adam stare at each other with enthusiastic intensity.

Maybe the two of us have special abilities! Jane thinks to herself with pride. *Adam and I are in with the popular kids and we are more special than they are!*

Then Jane asks, "Has anything visible ever appeared at one of your meetings before? That would be super awesome!"

"No," Selah responds, "but our power must be getting stronger, so that means that it could be possible any time now!"

"You don't think that he was foolin' around with us, do you?" asks Wes.

"No! That was too real!" Adam responds.

"Hey!" Daniel pipes in. "Let's go to the pizza and ice cream place to celebrate!"

The others agree. David follows behind, confused with fear. The beast of deception and darkness has been invited to Rocky Water by fools who know not what they have done.

CHAPTER 12

The remaining part of the summer, the group of "sorcerers," which they now call themselves, continues to meet with each other. They meet at Annie the dragon every night with the Ouija board until school starts in the fall, after which they return to Friday night séances with Mr. Potiphar at the beach shack. Eventually, they give up Saturday nights at the speedway to meet with Mr. Potiphar, who has changed since that night of the cold chill in the haunted shack. He's very somber, and he tells them about the newest scary "Slasher" movie he has seen. He also gives them an assignment: plan the perfect murder—in theory—and share the plot with the other members of the elite group.

David thinks it is a strange request, but does his assignment.

Reinforcement of Annie, the dragon, is completed the last week of October, just in time for Halloween. Selah and Jane invite Josie to join them for her first time that "All Hallows Eve" and introduce her to their coven circle of fellow witches and wizards.

Josie becomes a regular member of the "coven" by Thanksgiving, when she introduces them to a new business in town called The Wizard's Hall. Here they discover Tarot cards, with which Josie quickly becomes adept at reading, interpreting the future of whoever sits across the table from her. "I'm good at divination!" she says proudly.

One day, Josie is alone with Faith because Esther had another unexpected crisis in the garden club to which she had to call a meeting. The two were alone, sitting at the dining room table, and Josie wanted to tell Faith's future with the Tarot cards.

"Sweetie, let's not do that right now, because I need to talk to you."

"OK, Mrs. Wilson." Josie places the cards back into the box.

"You told me a little about what you and Selah and Jane have been doing together at Dragon Point. You're almost eight years old now, and you're very smart for your age. I want to tell you something that I didn't know before, and I think you should know it, too."

Josie pushes the box of cards to the side and leans forward with her elbows on the table, face in her hands, to look contemplatively at Faith.

"I'm concerned that you and your family, and Jane and Adam also, have stopped going to church with me on Sundays. Can you tell me why? You and I have always been able to talk about many things. You know you can trust me with this, too."

Josie thinks for a moment. "I don't feel good when I'm in the church."

"You don't feel good in what way?"

"Every time I listen to a sermon, especially when I hear the words in the Scripture reading, my tummy starts to hurt and I'm afraid that I'm gonna throw up." [1]

Faith is a little stunned at what she hears.

"Thank you for being honest with me, Josie; and now I'm going to be honest with you."

Immediately, Faith stands up, walks to the television cabinet and pulls out Stephen's notebook.

Josie's eyes are wide with surprise as she covers her mouth with both hands.

"Did Jane tell you about it, Mrs. W? It was our secret."

"No, I saw it that first day you showed it to Jane. I overheard you from the kitchen."

Josie sits quietly, filled with anticipation.

Finally, Faith begins with, "I recently found out from Stephen, in his notes here," she points with trembling finger, "that there is a lot I don't know about the Bible. I go to church, and I'm a good person, but that's not all there is to getting to heaven."

Josie is silent and attentive.

"Stephen says that there are certain activities that some people engage in that God is angry about; so if you do these things, you won't get to heaven when you die. I don't mean to frighten you, but it's very important that you hear what I have to say, so I want you to listen carefully, OK? Because I care about you very much."

Josie's face expresses curious anticipation.

"Remember that Jesus is the *true* light?" Opening the notebook she says, "Listen to what Jesus says: 'All who do evil hate the light and will not come to the light, because it will show all the evil things they do. But those who follow the true way come to the light... (John 3:19-21 NCV).'" She continues to speak to the wide-eyed little girl sitting at her table. "The true way is studying and doing what Jesus teaches in the Bible. Any other way is a road of lies leading directly into Satan's trap, like a lion crouching in the bushes to sneak up on a wildebeest, their favorite prey. Remember seeing that on the Nature shows?"

Faith looks at Josie. She notices that the child is holding her stomach and her face is pale.

"My tummy hurts. I think I'm gonna throw up."

Faith sets the notebook down and helps Josie to the bathroom. When she is finished, Josie says, "I'm better now."

Faith checks Josie's forehead. "You don't have a fever."

"Mrs. W, try reading again."

"OK, if you're sure you're all right."

"Yeah, I am. Please, read."

"Satan doesn't want us to read the truth in the Bible. Do you want to know what God says is the truth? In Deuteronomy chapter eighteen, verses ten and eleven, God implores us," Josie, listen: "Let no one... be found...who practices...sorcery...engages in witchcraft, or casts spells or who...consults the dead. Anyone who does these things is detestable to the Lord.'"

When Faith looks up, Josie is smiling.

"I'm all better now. It didn't make me sick to listen to the Scriptures!" Then a look of somber consternation comes over her face. "What happened to me, Mrs. W?"

Faith takes a deep breath and lets it out slowly. "Did you hear what I just read?"

"Yeah, that sorcery and witchcraft are things that God doesn't like us to do."

"I think that deep in your mind, your conscience knows that what you are doing is wrong. You and the others, without knowing what the results would be, have opened a portal into the supernatural realm, the 'dark side of the force'. Do you understand what I'm saying?"

Eyes wide with awe and excitement, Josie nods her head. "Yes! I know! It's like the magical portal to get on the Hogwarts Express! When Harry found out about the invisible portal, he had to walk through it without stopping or being afraid! Everyone else walked right by it without knowing that there *was* a door to a magical realm!" [2]

"Yes! But *Harry Potter* is a make-believe story. A lot of people don't know that there is only one way to reach the heavenly realm of God, through Jesus' door. We can't see the door, or God, but we have faith that He is there on the other side, and this is real, not fantasy like the books. We must be absolutely sure that we don't get on the wrong road and open the wrong door. Jesus calls it a *gate.* Where is it in Stephen's notes? Here it is. 'The way to get to heaven: "Enter through the narrow gate. The gate is wide and the road is wide that leads to hell, and many people enter through that gate. But the gate is small and the road is narrow that leads to true life. Only a few people find that road."' [3]

"Isn't it sad, Josie, that not many will find the correct road and discover how to get to heaven? In the first book, didn't Harry search for the sorcerer's stone that had the power of immortality?"[4] Faith waits for Josie to recall.

"What is a stone or a rock like?" Faith asks. "It's very hard and it lasts forever; it doesn't wither and die like a flower, does it?"

"Jesus is like that stone in *Harry Potter,* Josie. He possesses the power of immortality for people who find Him. The rock of immortality can only be found on the narrow road. And just think, Josie, this stone is not make-believe as in those books, this one is real! Don't you feel sad for all the people who are lost on the wide road and don't even know that they are lost, or that there *is* a stone that has power to give them immortality?"

"Should we tell people that there really is a stone that can be found that has powers of immortality?" asked Josie.

"Yes, Josie. Those of us who know that we are on the correct path, out of concern for others, desire to tell them how dangerous the wide road is, so we tell them about the rock called Jesus."

"Then why don't people listen when they hear about the narrow road and the rock?" Josie was confused.

"Because we can't prove to them that it's real, only God can. If they *truly* want to find the stone and the small gate on the narrow path, they'll search for it. Just as Harry had to walk through a wall without hesitating or being scared, we Christians must walk in faith without fear or giving up on trying to convince others about the wrong path that they are on. Most people won't listen, but we can't give up trying to help them. God wants everyone to find His road so that everybody can have immortality."

Josie decides to tell Faith a secret. "Do you know what Stephen said, once, before he died? He made up a short saying. Let me see if I can remember his exact words. 'God asks all of us for a day of worship; He desires our devotion for a lifetime; He receives only a few for eternity.'"

Faith gazes lovingly at her little friend, who is smiling at her from across the table.

"That was very profound of him, and wonderful that you remembered it. So what do you think you should do differently after what you've learned today?"

Josie takes only a moment to think. "If God says that playing around with witchcraft and sorcery will keep me from heaven, then I don't want to do it anymore. I want to go to heaven with you, Mrs. Wilson. Are you going to tell the others what you've told me today so that they will want to stop doing those evil things, too? I want them to be in heaven with us. Mommy doesn't do bad things. She's a good person, right? Does that mean that she will be allowed to go to heaven?"

"Remember, it takes more than being a good person to be saved when one is on the wrong path. One must ask God to be saved and trust Him by following *all truth* to the small gate. That's faith. Every time we read the Bible and learn more about what God wants us to do, our faith grows stronger, along with our desire to stay on the narrow path and learn about the true way. I've already told your mommy about Jesus. Some people will listen."

"I'm so glad about that. I hope that Selah, Jane, David and Adam will listen." Then Josie does something unexpected. She jumps up from her chair, snatches the deck of Tarot cards from the table, and walks into the kitchen.

As she tosses the deck of cards into the trash can, she sees someone out of the corner of her eye sitting on the kitchen floor. "Jared! What are you doing here? You scared me!"

Faith hears Josie and enters the kitchen. She walks over to Jared and sits on the floor with him. "Jared? You haven't been to visit me for awhile. Why didn't you join us at the dining room table when you came in the back door?"

Up to this point, Jared has been staring at the floor. As he raises his eyes to meet Faith's gaze, he answers, "I have to tell you what Adam has told me about the séances. After overhearing what you and Josie were talking about, we have to do something to stop him."

"Stop who? Stop Adam?"

"No…Satan."

"He's right." Startled, Faith and Josie turn to see Paul standing in the doorway to the kitchen. "And you were right, too, Faith. I'm so sorry."

Faith jumps up and runs to embrace her husband.

CHAPTER 13

After Esther picks up Josie a few minutes later, Jared recounts the occurrence at the session of the coven which Adam had told him about two days ago. "I think that Mr. Potiphar is full of evil, and it scares me. Adam seems so proud that he's part of all of this. I told my dad what I know. When Adam finds out, he'll never speak to me again."

Then Paul adds, "Don't feel as though you have betrayed Adam, Jared. You did the right thing telling your dad, because this is something dangerous that's going on."

Faith looks at Paul with concern. "You know more, don't you?"

Jared stands up from the table. "I'm glad that, since Selah isn't a cheerleader this year, my sister Donna doesn't hang with her anymore. I believe you two have a lot to talk about, so I'll see you later."

"Tell your dad, thank you very much for calling me about this."

With a forlorn countenance, Jared nods and walks out the back door.

"Paul, I'm so happy that you've come back. You were so mad at me and adamant about the 'problem' that had arisen between us. What changed your mind?"

"How it happened is so incredible, really. I ran into Jared's father, Simon Preston, one night at a restaurant, so we had dinner together. We never said much to each other before that night because I didn't want to have anything to do with him. I tried to avoid him at the office, because I knew that he was an elder of the church, and I didn't want to be preached to. Oh, he was always subtle about his religion; I heard this from my other co-workers who *hadn't* been able to avoid him," Paul conveys with a slight smile; an affectionate smile, Faith thinks. "I now admit that he is the most interesting man that I've ever met. I told him right away that first night at the restaurant that I grew up Catholic and that I didn't need to be saved. It was *that* place of rituals that bored me with God, so I had no interest in knowing Him. You and I talked about how I felt about God, and all that stuff, on our very first date, remember?"

"Yes, I do. You were ecstatic that I was indifferent about the subject, too."

"So, you can understand then, when out of nowhere, after Stephen died, you began to tell me about what had happened to you, how you had 'found Jesus.' Stephen's death hit me like a five-ton truck and I didn't need to hear *your* news on top of that."

Faith notices another slight smile lace through Paul's eyes. She reaches forward across the table and, with much love in *her* eyes, squeezes his hand.

Paul says, "For the last six months, I've been doing a lot of thinking and a whole bunch of studying with Simon. I'm born again! How, I can't even begin to tell you!"

"You don't have to. I understand why you can't because I went through it, too. True conversion is a different experience for everyone, and it is a secret between you and God. You feel like a completely new person when you are 'born again.'"

"And I understand something now," Paul admits. "The truth makes you feel so amazing that you want to share it with everyone, even strangers! It's such good news that it's hard **not** to want everyone to have Him in their lives too! Thank you for sticking with me through my stubborn pride, Faith. I know now why you had to tell me about Jesus."

Then he takes a deep breath. "Now, it's high time that we do something about our kids before they join Wicca.[1] They've been up in Cassadaga, Florida, the haven for 'New Agers' who live by the occultic practices of psychics, sorcerers, séance mediums and all that evil stuff. Were you aware?"

A look of surprise comes to Faith's face. "Oh, no! I didn't know that they had been there! I just found out from Stephen's journal that sorcery and witchcraft are evil in the eyes of God." She puts her face in her hands for a moment and tears come to her eyes. "This is my fault for not paying more attention to what they have been doing. Adam and Jane are thrilled to be friends with Selah and Daniel Windfeather." She looks at Paul. "How can we explain how dangerous this path is without pushing them away from us?"

"I've spoken to both Jane and Adam on the phone, and neither one of them has told me that they have been associating with Daniel Windfeather. He and David Abrams are both part of a gang in town. The cops are keeping their eyes on the two of them in an ongoing bike theft investigation. Did you know that Jane had her bike stolen?"

"No. How do you know all of this? I had a feeling that you knew more, but didn't want to say anything in front of Jared."

"I've been keeping in touch with John Abrams. As mayor, he's kept informed about what goes on in town; and as our neighbor, he kept me updated about how you were while I was getting right with God." With a pause, he adds, "I know that Jared knows more than he told us tonight. I need to talk with him."

Faith gets up and walks over to her husband. She puts her arms around him. "I love you, Paul."

"I love you, too. Now what is this about Stephen's journal? What journal?"

Later that night, Jane and Adam are thankful that their mother is already in bed for the night. They don't know that their dad is back.

"Adam, we've never stayed out this late on a school night, before," whispers Jane. "It's an hour past our curfew; usually Mom stays up and waits for us to get back."

"Yeah! Our spell-casting powers are really working! Selah told me about the first time she used one on her mom. Three more days of lousy school, then winter break!"

"You mean 'Christmas break'. This 'politically correct' language is irritating, so we don't offend anyone. What about offending God by not saying 'Merry Christmas' even! It's like a slap in His face to ignore Him!"

"Okay, okay! Wow! What a 'Bible thumper' you are!"

"Shhh! Don't wake her! I'm going to bed and I suggest you do the same."

"Yes, Madam Sorceress!"

David's nightmare is longer this time. He can't move as the hot, foul breath is heavy on his neck. The substance of the darkness that surrounds him is like black tar. He is unable to think as he tries to focus in on the animal that is upon his neck. Now, he feels teeth touching both sides of his throat. He tries with all his might to see in the darkness. *Please let me see where I am!*

Suddenly, there are flashes of lightning. *The dragon! It's the dragon!* he realizes as it pulls back from him in the light. Suddenly, David can't believe his eyes --- the monster transmutates into a lion with a thick, black mane. Its snarled lips reveal blood-wrapped gigantic teeth. He still can't move. He can barely breathe in the putrid fumes surrounding him.

Slowly, the choking darkness that crushes the air out of him lightens slowly so that he can watch the lion lift its head above where David is cowering in the dirt. It glowers down at him. David is able to see as he glances quickly around his surroundings that he is in a large cave filled with deep caverns, one of which he is on the edge.

He takes his eyes off the lion's demonic scowl momentarily to quickly back away from the dark abyss in front of him. His back hits a large boulder. He's cornered!

Then, all of a sudden, the lion mutates into an angelic being emanating sparkling luminescence. The beautiful, softly lit being speaks. "Why do you look so frightened of me? I'm here to help you find your way. Stand up child, and follow me. Take my hand."

As the being holds out his hand to him, David is mesmerized by his gentle coercion, and raises his hand to meet his.

Unexpectedly, David sees Adam appear, with a look of fear frozen on his face, behind the being. The angelic being turns slowly to look into Adam's eyes.

David attempts to pull his hand back, but he is unable to. It's as though his arm is filled with lead. David's whole body fills with intense fear as he watches the angel turn back into what he really is: a repulsive serpent. Once again, before his eyes, the serpent transforms into the lion. The giant beast explodes with evil fury and rams his head into Adam, knocking him off his feet. Then it lunges toward his prone body with its mouth wide open.

Jane awakens during the night and rubs her throat, which is very sore and raw. Immediately, she realizes that she has a fever. "Mom," calls Jane in a raspy voice.

Jane's bedroom door is open; Faith hears the call. She gets up and runs in and sits on Jane's bed. She enfolds her daughter in her arms and recognizes that Jane has a scorching fever. Faith leaves the room to get some aspirin and a glass of water.

Through her tear-filled vision, Jane sees her father in the doorway. "Dad? Oh, Daddy!"

He hurriedly runs to embrace his daughter. "Janie, I've missed you so much. I'll never leave again. I promise."

CHAPTER 14

By the fourth day, Jane feels much better. It's a week before Christmas. *I'm so glad that I had finished my shopping and gift-wrapping before I got sick.*

The next day, Faith feels comfortable enough to leave Adam with his sister, who is almost completely recovered from an undiagnosed infection. Paul and Faith want to go out on a date, and Adam is quite pleased.

"Dad, I'm happy that you're back, but get out of here!" Adam quips jokingly. "We'll be fine. I'll take good care of my little big sister. Go on your date."

When they reach the car, Paul and Faith decide to discuss over dinner the pressing issue of the evil which has crept deceitfully into their family life.

"We'll determine the best way to approach this," declares Paul. "We'll visit Jared and Simon Preston first to find out all that Jared knows. They're expecting us, so let's go over there; then, I'll take my beautiful wife to her favorite Italian restaurant beachside."

"I've got a surprise for you, my short-of-stature sister," says Adam.

As Adam brings out his cell phone, Jane inquisitively shrieks, "What? Who are you calling?"

"All is clear and ready for take-off," he says to the person on the other end of the connection, then hangs up. "Ya might wanna brush your hair, Sis. It looks like a rumpled bird's nest."

"Oh, thank you very much for your concern about my appearance. Who's coming over?" Jane inquires as she gets up to "unrumple" herself.

"You will discover very soon, so get yourself presentable to meet your guests."

Ten minutes later, the sorcerers' coven assembles together at the dining room table in the Wilson home. At 6 p.m., it is completely dark inside, except for a large candle in the middle of the table.

Jane is quite proud that her friends don't want to leave her out of their meeting. *What good luck that Mom and Dad aren't expected back for some time!* There is excitement in the air as the session begins. *The incense smells wonderful,* Jane thinks as she looks around at all of her friends. *I wonder why Josie didn't want to come to this special meeting.*

Mr. Potiphar begins with, "An auspicious occurrence will befall us tonight, ladies and gentlemen. Concentrate." He speaks slowly and with confidence. "Close your eyes and breathe deeply the aroma of the wizard's smoke. Enter into the transition state in order to obtain connection with the spirits. Who is near us in the invisible realm tonight? Join us, departed one."

They all hum quietly in harmonized tones, and wait.

David opens his eyes, and detects an unnerving aura about Mr. Potiphar this evening. He peers at each of the faces around him in an attempt to determine if anyone else feels the thickness of the air in the room. His heart begins to race. He closes his eyes again, calms down, and concentrates like he has been taught to do.

Mr. Potiphar is the first to sense the presence. He opens his eyes to view the appearance of the entity. He greets the ghost with a soft and slow voice. "Welcome, kind spirit. Everyone, be still. Brothers and sisters, open your eyes. Don't move."

At this announcement, they all open their eyes to gaze upon a hazy spirit form that stands between David and Jane. In their peripheral vision, Jane and David watch nervously as the figure steps an inch closer to the table.

Jane manages to turn her head. She breathes rapidly as terror fills her chest. As she clamps tightly onto Adam's hand on her left and David's hand on her right, Adam and his sister look into the face of their dead brother, Stephen.

They both quiver with fright as they stare at the apparition. It suddenly does something very strange. The ghost of Stephen reaches out to David to take his hand, and at the same time he places a translucent, black kerchief over his own face. David, trembling, extends his arm to the haunting specter and tentatively grabs its hand. Immediately, David feels in his grip something like electrically-charged spider webs which cover a skeletal hardness beneath.[1]

Jane begins to moan with fear as she watches the scene unfold. This sound causes the ghost to turn to Jane and smile. She sees a perfect image of Stephen's smile through the thin, translucent veil, a smile that she knows very well. They all stare with open mouths and quiver at what they are witnessing.

The next few moments seem to happen in slow motion. Seemingly out of nowhere, Jared and Josie appear in the room with the group at the table. This intrusion infuriates Mr. Potiphar and the ghost. The ghost of Stephen snatches the kerchief from his face and throws it on the floor. Then he morphs into something half animal, half human.[2] Jane hears Josie and Jared speaking, but it is drowned by a deep, rumbling snarl that emanates from the half beast, half man.

At the same instant, Mr. Potiphar's face slowly distorts. His jaw seems to come unhinged. He lifts one leg in the air and holds it there at an inhuman angle. Suddenly, he lets out a ferocious, ear-piercing scream. When it ceases, the group hears Jared and Josie speaking Scripture as they hold each other's hands. Each of them has their other hand extended toward both the demonic spirit and the demon-possessed man, who continues to contort his body into incredible distorted positions.

Josie quotes from the Bible: "I will fear no evil, for **JESUS** is with me. Thy rod and thy staff…"[3]

Then Jared is heard to say, "The Lord God Almighty rebukes you, Satan! **JESUS** is our Lord and mighty defender of our salvation through His blood! The blood of **JESUS**. Victory belongs to **JESUS**! Hear me! You are doomed Satan! Depart this place in the name of **JESUS**. In the powerful, holy name of **JESUS**, I command you to leave, **NOW!**"

Jared continues his barrage of commands, but then, suddenly, he falls to his knees, raises his arms to the ceiling and requests, "Holy Father, open the eyes of their hearts and minds so that they may see your glorious sovereignty that is with us!" His face is aglow with divine brightness.

Suddenly, a tall warrior in battle attire manifests and stands in front of Jared and Josie. He has a fierce countenance, eyes of fire and feet of burning bronze.[4]

Everyone at the table except Mr. Potiphar falls to the floor in trembling weakness. In fear of the warrior, the ghost dematerializes. Mr. Potiphar slowly disengages from the impossible, inhuman contortions into which the demon had forced him. The demon screams, jerks the man's body violently, and Mr. Potiphar's head hits the edge of the table as he is slammed to the floor.

David, Daniel, Selah, Adam and Jane are unable to move in their state of weakness on the floor. Their eyes are wide with a terror they've never known before as they watch the angelic warrior stare directly at them with complete sadness and disappointment in his eyes. Then He disappears.

Jared picks up Josie into his arms. "We did it! Well, Jesus' power did it, not us. He used us to exorcise the evil out of here! Can you believe it, Josie? Jesus came!" They embrace each other in victory as the others are mute in their disbelief.

It is then that Josie sees the Wilsons standing in the doorway that leads into the kitchen. Their mouths are agape with incredulity. Josie points them out to Jane and Adam, with a big smile on her face as Jared lifts her from the floor and swings her in a circle.

Faith and Paul run over to the cowering teens and bend down to comfort them. "It's all right now," Faith coos softly as she gently strokes the head of each terrified teen. They come out of their stupor and get reassuring hugs from both adults. Josie clings to Adam, who holds her tightly in his arms.

Paul assists all of them to their feet. "Here. Sit down." He leads them to the living room, offering them seats on the soft couch and chairs.

Paul looks over at his wife and kids to assure that they are okay. He places his head in his hands as he sits on the arm of the chair where Faith is seated. He lets out a deep breath, which he realizes he has been holding since walking into the house and witnessing a supernatural occurrence that caused a fearsome trembling through his entire body. He still trembles slightly as he sits down.

Paul then becomes aware of the man who lies unconscious near the table on the dining room floor. He quickly reaches him and checks for a pulse. He detects it and checks to make sure that the man is breathing.

"He's alive. I'm calling 911."

Paul rushes to the phone in the living room, dials 911, and then almost drops the receiver. There, on the floor between the chairs that David and Jane had occupied just moments ago, lies a black kerchief.

CHAPTER 15

The teens stare, dumbfounded and unable to move, only able to tremble with fear. They also see the kerchief, but they don't mention it to the others. Not a word is said until after the ambulance has taken away Mr. Potiphar.

Paul closes the front door and walks over to where Faith sits. He releases a deep sigh and sits on the large arm of the chair next to his wife. Jane is sitting on the floor with her head in her mother's lap. Adam glares at Jared with a look of contempt.

"Why did you intrude, Jared? You ruined everything!"

Jared says nothing, but returns a look of surprised confusion toward Adam.

Paul admonishes his son. "Adam! You obviously have no idea how dangerous what you have just done really is, do you! These two very possibly have just saved your lives!"

Adam angrily jumps up from the couch, stomps out and slams his bedroom door.

Paul continues admonishing the others. "I want to know what possessed all of you to engage in such stupid behavior! Didn't you know that you were inviting evil into your lives? You opened the door and invited Satan right in!"

"Paul!" interjects Faith. "I think we should profusely thank Jared and Josie for being brave enough to do what they did." She looks around at the teens in her living room. "They told us what you all were planning tonight. That's why we came back."

Paul, still visibly angry, says, "I have half a notion to press multiple charges of contributing to the delinquency of a minor against that…pea brain…Mr. Potiphar," he stutters as he points to the front door.

Jared inquires, "May I say something, Mr. Wilson, Mrs. Wilson?"

Faith nods with a look of newfound respect for her young friend.

"There are so many people who have no idea that what they're doing is something sinful that God forbids anyone to do. Whatever is against God is sin, whether you believe it or not. Truth is still the truth, whether you believe it or not. Some of the books we read, the violent video games we play or movies we watch, bombard our minds and desensitize us to evil. The whole world begins to call society's acceptance of evil, 'tolerance of others,' or 'political correctness,' as though there were no right and wrong anymore; so those who don't know Jesus and what is in the Bible think that anything they do is OK; but *God* says it's sinful. Satan is called 'the prince of this world' and he has God's permission to influence us as he pleases because Adam and Eve made the choice to disobey God. So, Satan is the ruler of this world. Jesus said: 'If you are not with me, then you are against me.'"[1]

Josie chimes in with a lesson of her own. "So that means you won't get to heaven if you're not with Jesus, huh, Jared? Everyone is on one side or the other."

He simply smiles at her with warmth, and then studies the others' faces to determine if they are listening and allowing things to soak in. He notices that Paul and Faith are both smiling tenderly his way. Jared continues, "Everybody saw what just happened here. You know that the supernatural world is *very* real. Why would anyone choose to reject Jesus and His teachings to jump headlong into a relationship with demons? If the 'dark side' is real, then God is real. Isn't that a logical deduction?

"Jesus said in Matthew chapter eighteen, 'that if two of you on earth pray about something together,' like Josie and I did, that 'it will be done for you by my Father in heaven…because if two or three people come together in my name, I am there with you.' And you all saw Him."

The teens in the room stare at each other with disbelief. "That was Jesus?" asks Daniel.

Jared slowly nods. "Jesus isn't a little baby lying in a manger anymore."

The teens are incredulous.

"I have to say something else here," adds Paul. "These things that you have been 'practicing' are not make believe. Witchcraft and sorcery are real forms of false religion that a great number of people are tricked into believing and practicing. Some of these people think that their way is the path to 'oneness' with God; but God *is not pleased* at all with what they are doing, because everything He wants us to discover is in the Bible, which is full of His Word of salvation. There's only *one* way to heaven --- that's having faith in Jesus and what He did for us on the cross. That's all part of the truth that Satan wants to keep hidden from those who don't desire to seek Jesus or have any interest in the Bible."

Paul directs his gaze at each one in the room, and lastly at Faith when he finishes what he had to say. She smiles with pleasure at all that he has learned while he was away.

Paul asks, "Do you really think that Stephen was here tonight? If you do, then you were deceived by Satan. He'll do anything that it takes to draw you away from the real truth you must search for; and he has plenty of demons to assist him in carrying out his malicious, devious plans. You have been made fools of by Satan."

"Do you realize," inserts Faith, "that you all quit going to the teen center, the skating rink, the speedway *and* to church? And," says Faith as she looks at Jane, "how long has it been since you sang? You dropped out of the choir this year at school *and* at church. Furthermore, Selah, you dropped out of cheerleading, something that I know you enjoy. In fact, and I say this to all of you, you stopped all of your wholesome activities that you truly enjoy doing, and are now totally doing what Satan wants you to do --- which is to forget about what Jesus has done for all of us. You have sided with the devil. All of your spare time is spent..." She hesitates a moment to find the right words "in learning the 'dark side of the force.' Never! and I mean *never,* underestimate Satan's ability to keep you from finding God. He's much smarter than you could ever imagine. He's tricked all of you into following him, so your interest is drawn away from God and His holy truth. All of your time has been practicing unholy things because Satan has made sure of that. You are in his trap, and he has kept you in the dark so you can't see that he has your souls in the palm of his hand, and you aren't even aware of it."

After a moment's hesitation, Jane asks, "Do you mean that we are 'Satan worshipers'?"

Faith simply stares at her, and then glances slowly around to all of them without saying a word.

"So…" Daniel concludes, "If I don't *choose* to be on God's side, then I'm on Satan's side by default?" His face holds an expression of bewilderment.

"That's just insane and it's not true," snaps Selah with disrespect. Up to this point she and David have been silent.

David agrees with Selah. "C'mon, Faith, I know that we are *not* Satan worshipers; you're exaggerating to be dramatic because you're scared to explore the paranormal."

"You see!" Jared points out. "You *can't* believe the truth, even when it's directly in front of your eyes, because Satan has tricked you! Have you forgotten what just happened here tonight? Doesn't it prove that there is a loving God? One of the secrets that Satan and his demons don't want you to know about the supernatural world is that you are joining *his* side by not knowing the truth: that your sins keep you from God, and if you don't intentionally choose to repent of your sins and ask for forgiveness to join God's side, then you are on Satan's side. The evil spirits want to fascinate you with their end of the invisible world, the dark side, so you won't discover the opposite end, where there is light by which to see the truth. You can't see in the dark, can you? It's as if you were blind *and* brainwashed. Your minds are blocked while you sin on Satan's side."

David speaks after a long-held silence laden with everyone's thoughts. "Are you saying that, if we now decide to switch sides, our sight and our minds will be 'unblocked'?"

"Yes!" answers Jared with excitement. "It will be too late after death to be saved."

"Saved? Saved from what, Jared? Don't go over the deep end and start <u>preaching</u> to us," David warns.

"Isn't that what he's been doing?" Selah retorts, "Preaching?"

Jared answers, "You *need* to hear it; every one of you. Don't you guys get it?" he admonishes, looking around at their faces. "Don't you believe in God? Wouldn't you rather live like there *is* a God, and discover that there isn't, than to live like there *isn't* a God, and then, after you die, discover that there *is* a powerful God who will judge you? By then it will be too late to change sides."

Another moment of complete quiet follows Jared's declaration.

With a quick movement, Faith reaches into her large handbag and pulls out a maroon-colored notebook, unzips it, and prepares to read.

Jane's face expresses surprise and confusion as she looks over at Josie. *Did you tell Mom about it?* her expression seems to imply.

Josie slowly shakes her head in answer to Jane's unspoken inquiry.

Faith changes her mind. She extends the notebook to her daughter. Jane returns a loving smile to her mother as she allows the notebook to gently slide into her hands, then smiling shyly as she opens it.

"Stephen titled this, 'Children Walking in Truth.' He paraphrased some Scriptures, as though he were reminded of them while writing down his thoughts." She begins to read,

"'It is beyond our mental capacity to imagine the power of God. He inspired the minds of the authors of the Bible to write down His knowledge so we could learn about the concealed truths of God's promises and gifts of His power. (Romans 15:4) The deep concepts of the truth can be discovered, but only if we search for and learn the knowledge He left for us. Only those who sincerely desire to learn God's truth in the lighted end of the supernatural realm, and sincerely believe, will be led "into all truth." (John 16:13)'"

Jane continues to read from her brother's notebook:

"'The dead are in their graves, not somewhere in another dimension as disembodied spirits or ghosts. After death, the conscience of the person who died is in an *un*conscious sleep. In the book of Ecclesiastes (a Greek word for "one who addresses an assembly," Webster's New World Dictionary), chapter 9, verses 5 and 6 states: "The living know that they will die, but the dead know nothing... their love, hate and their jealousy have...vanished; never again will they have a part in anything under the sun." (NIV). To express it another way: they are not aware of anything that happens here in the world. In John's Gospel, Jesus calls death "sleep." Why would Jesus raise Lazarus from death if his friend were already in heaven? Lazarus was in a dreamless state of sleep from which Jesus returned him to life. If Lazarus had gone immediately to heaven, Jesus wouldn't be so callous as to take Lazarus out of heaven!

"'So, if ghosts aren't our friends and loved ones who have died, who or what are they? They are demons! There have been many documented accounts of sightings of apparitions during séances and in "haunted buildings," so we know that they are real. If *they* are real, then God must be real also. We all are designed with curiosity about the supernatural, but most people tend to steer toward the dark end. That's "spiritualism": the belief that the dead survive as spirits which can communicate with the living. (Webster's New World Dictionary). Why do people tend to contact the dark end of the invisible world? Because Satan makes it easy to contact his side. It's so much easier to invite evil into one's life than to sincerely desire to invite Jesus into one's heart and learn how to live a holy life. He's always at the door knocking, waiting for you to invite Him in. (Revelation 3:20).'"

Jane stops reading and raises her eyes to the others in the room.

"That's all well and good and all that... gobbledygook," David suddenly blurts out. "But I still want to know what 'saved' means. Saved from *what*? And why would God conceal information that He wants us to have? The Bible is *so* screwed up and full of contradictions. It's too complicated for anyone but a genius to understand."

Paul and Faith both look at each other with the same idea. Suddenly, Paul makes a request. "May we interrupt for just a moment, Janie? We would like Adam to hear this also."

It takes a lot of cajoling, but Adam emerges with a sullen face.

"Listen," Jane begins, "Listen to what Stephen wrote here. 'From *The Prayer Key New Testament* by Rex Humbard, page 176:

'To many the Bible is a puzzle. Some find it hard reading and thus refuse to spend time with the Word. Most often this is merely an excuse of the carnal man keeping him from the discipline of the Word. The Bible *can* be understood. However, only a very special group of people can understand the Word.
(Emphasis mine)'"

"THERE! You see!" David interrupts while he emphatically leans forward on the couch. 'Only a very special group of people can understand' the Bible. I told you!"

"She didn't get to finish because she was rudely interrupted," Jared rebukes.

David leans back in his seat with a sigh and crosses his arms in front of his chest.

Jane continues reading:

"'It is hidden from the unbeliever. Man through his own wisdom does not know God. (1 Corinthians 1:21). Man simply cannot through his own intelligence save himself. Thus, to the man who does not believe in Christ, the Bible remains a puzzle. (1 Corinthians 1:19)'"

"May I clarify something before you go on?" Jared inquires of Jane, who nods her head in acquiescence. "David, you asked why God would conceal information from us in the Bible. It's concealed from unbelievers, those who don't accept Jesus as the one who offered his life to save our souls from annihilation. Only those who have the Holy Spirit can understand what God is saying in His Bible. *Saved* means you will be with God after you die. Everyone's soul will live in the afterlife and will appear before God on the Day of Judgment. Until then, those who have died are in their graves awaiting the Day of Judgment when God raises them from the dead. Those souls who aren't saved will be judged as sinners when they are awakened. Their punishment in hell is brief but full of anguish for them, because they have realized too late what a terrible mistake they have made by not choosing God's side while they were alive. Sorrowfully, since the *un*saved would be miserable around all the saved believers, God mercifully destroys the unsaved soul ***and*** their consciousness. So, *saved* means that your soul won't be destroyed; you'll enjoy an after-life filled with joy through eternity! And we'll get to see God's face! God is full of love and desires that everyone be saved. He doesn't want to kill anyone's soul!

"There are two things that one must do to be saved: (1) repent of your sins—*stop doing them!* And (2) trust Jesus as your Savior; trust that He died to take *your* penalty. We all need a savior because we *all* are born *full* of sin."

"Whoa, whoa! Wait a minute!" David demands. "Babies and children are innocent, not sinful! You can't tell me that they go to hell when they die!" He exudes an air of defiant arrogance and pride which escapes no one's attention in the room. "Answer that one, 'Bible Thumpers!' Would a fair, loving God send children—who haven't even had time to sin yet in their young lives—into hell?"

Faith stares directly at David. "Just stop and think a moment, David. Aren't babies demanding and self-centered? Don't toddlers push and hit to steal a toy from each other? What child won't lie to keep themselves from being punished? Right there are two sins: stealing and lying. Have you ever stolen anything?"

Adam recalls the theft at the mall. Adam and David each avert their eyes downward, away from the others. David clears his throat in uneasiness.

Faith surveys each face as she asks, "Has anyone here ever told a lie? Even little 'white lies' count as sinful from God's point of view." She raises her eyebrows slightly as she waits for an answer from anyone; but no responses are forthcoming.

"So, do you see now that we *all* are in need of a Savior?" Faith continues, "We must first realize that we are sinners according to God's standards, and need His gift of salvation. And that's exactly what it is, a gift; but you must pray to Him and ask for it. You can't earn salvation by being a good person, going to church, or doing good deeds for others. Jesus said, 'I tell you the truth, no one can see the kingdom of God unless he is born again.'"[2] Faith notices that everyone is looking directly at her, all but Adam.

Adam refuses to listen and believe. He folds his arms tightly across his chest with a scowl on his face. His eyes congeal into pools of blackness; his mind closes as a result of his hardened heart.

Once again Adam sees the black kerchief lying on the floor. *I've got to get that and save it as a souvenir of this incredible night that we contacted the realm of the dead!*

CHAPTER 16

The following afternoon, Adam is in possession of the black kerchief. He hadn't been able to believe his luck in acquiring it without anyone's knowledge last night. He simply got up while the others were in a heated discussion, kicked it into the kitchen, picked it up, placed it into his pocket, and came back out with a pitcher of hot chocolate and some cups for everyone.

"I have something to do before Mom and Dad get back from work," Adam tells Jane as he walks out the door. "I won't be long."

Jane is surprised at his abruptness. With food in her mouth, she is unable to ask where he is going.

Adam gets on his bike, passes by the city's recreation building and thinks, *Jared and I haven't played basketball together since that day in the mall.* He arrives at Dragon Point in ten minutes, directly east across the causeway from the recreation center to the island. He sees dark storm clouds forming over the ocean, which answers his unspoken question as to the reason it is abnormally hot this December afternoon.

Adam hides his bike and sneaks through the overgrown bushes that line the side of the large empty house, to where Annie stands in the back yard. He is met with a surprise.

"Hey! Well, if it ain't the devil's luck finding you two here!" Daniel and David each look at the other as if to ask, *did* you *invite him here?* Irked with Adam's arrival, Daniel looks at his watch and sees that it is almost 3:30. He quickly slams the lid down on a tackle box in front of him. "What are you doing here?" he asks with impatience.

"You've got to see this," Adam explains as he pulls out the black kerchief from his pocket and places it over his face. A sudden gust of wind blows it out of place, but he quickly grabs it before it flies into the river.

"Hey!" both David and Daniel say at the same time. "You got it?"

"I came here to put it in the dragon," Adam explains. "It belongs in our secret hideout with our other 'mementos of accomplishments.'"

"Well, I'm proud of you," says Daniel as he puts his arm around Adam's neck.

"So am I," adds David. "We didn't make a mistake recruiting *you* into our club. I'm so happy that you aren't a Jesus freak like Jared. Can you believe that heapin' load of trash he was preachin' to us last night?" He lowers his head and snorts in contempt at Jared.

Daniel and Adam simply look at each other in silence as another gust of wind blows across Dragon Point and swirls with an eerie sound between the three boys.

"That storm is coming any moment," David quips. "Let's say that we open the tackle box and do what we came here for." His foot slips on the rocks, but he is able to regain his balance. *Adam needs to learn to be tough like me, without fear,* David thinks.

A horrendous crack of thunder resounds overhead, startling each of them to react with a sudden jerk.

"You're gonna fish *now*?" inquires Adam with disbelief in his voice.

With a look of query, David searches Daniel's face for the "OK" to include Adam in their plans today. He receives a nod of acknowledgement from Daniel.

Adam goes over to the door in the belly of the dragon and holds it open for the other two. A blast of air almost rips the door from his hand. "C'mon!" yells Adam simultaneously with the next crack of thunder.

David and Daniel each have a large grin on their faces and remain in place. They don't make a move to the open door. They had not heard Adam's voice in the tumult.

"It'll work!" yells Daniel. "You first, David, just like I showed you!"

Adam is confused as he watches Daniel open the tackle box. It's not bait that is pulled out in Daniel's hand. It's a gun.

"Ain't this Glock a beauty?" asks David rhetorically as he looks at Adam. With a look of delight, David carefully takes the loaded gun into his grasp. *Watch and learn that guns aren't so bad in the right hands, Adam.*

Daniel looks to be sure there is no one else around. "Wait for the sound of thunder!" he orders.

David pulls back the slide on the weapon and lets it spring forward into locked position. Both hands are holding the gun as he aims it at his first target: the closest pillar, one of the many which supports the massive bridge to his left.

"Any second now," David says calmly. He holds his breath.

When the next thunderous crack sounds, he pulls the trigger. The force of the shot knocks his arms upward. *I forgot to brace for the recoil!*

There are no cars crossing westward on this side of the bridge who would be able to spot the trio on the point. He again takes aim with tension in his straightened arms awaiting the next clap of thunder. He fires at the cement pillar.

"Bull's-eye!" shouts David as small bits of cement splatter outward, blowing away in the wind of the fast-approaching storm.

David peers upward into the face of the mighty beast towering above him and imagines that it obeys his every command. He turns his gaze inland to the coastline across the river. He spies a brown pelican struggling against the wind just above the white caps of the churning water. He steps forward to the edge of the river and hears the waves slapping against the rocks. He places a foot on the rocks and discovers once again that they make for slippery footing.

Once he determines that he is steady and balanced on the algae-covered rocks, he takes aim at the pelican still suspended in mid-air over the water. David looks down the barrel of the gun. Instantly, as if on cue, an explosion detonates in the sky. A gust of wind tips David off balance. Both of his feet slip out from under him on the rocks. He fires the gun accidentally, so the bullet has a trajectory too high to hit the pelican, its intended target. Instinctively, he drops the weapon and places his hands behind him to lessen the impact of the fall. The momentum lands him on his back and he slams his head into the leg of the giant beast; the pain causes him to curse under his breath.

Daniel tries to catch his friend, but instead falls down with David against the trunk-like leg of the dragon. They both watch helplessly as the gun slides into the dark, churning water of the lagoon.

Adam has been frozen in a state of disbelief during this time, unable to move his lips in protest to the scenes as they unfold in front of him. *A maniac with a gun killed Stephen!*

Both David and Daniel sit stunned for a moment from the fierce blow they have received to the back of their heads. David has searing pain in his tailbone. He curses at the top of his lungs, the sound of which is shrouded in the deafening blast of thunder that rumbles through his chest. He rubs the back of his head, where he feels a swollen lump. Touching it causes him to clench his eyes closed and gasp in pain. Daniel raises himself to a sitting position and leans against the leg of the dragon. He then is able to assist David to sit upon his sore tailbone.

David slowly comes out of his state of painful bewilderment. He sees the empty shell casings near him in the sand. He reaches forward, gathers them, and tosses them into the river.

With the next crack of thunder, a glaring ray of lightning strikes a transformer on a nearby pole. Daniel pulls David to his feet and all three of them enter into the belly of the dragon for refuge from the onslaught of the storm, which is now directly overhead.

Selah pulls into the parking lot of Rocky Water Recreation and Civic Center to pick up Josie from her weekly baton lesson. She's ten minutes early, and her little sister will be coming out of the side door at 3:30 p.m. She watches Adam as he passes by on his bicycle.

Selah's eyes brim with tears after sobbing her heart out to Wes with the truth which she has been afraid to deal with for three months. It was confirmed one hour ago at the Women's Clinic – she's pregnant. She had gone over to tell Wes, who had stormed out of his front door after hearing the news.

"How could you let this happen, Selah?" he had bellowed. "You're on your own. I'm outta here." He had humiliated her and had broken her heart. Now all she could do was cry.

Selah wants very much to drive away so Josie can't see her like this. Her mind begins to whirl with visions of herself as an angry, horrible mother to the baby that she is not ready for. She gazes with blurred vision at the building where she and Donna Preston had taken their cheerleading lessons together when they were both Josie's age. *I guess college is out of the question. Daddy will be ashamed of me and my mother will never have her wish come true of me being Miss Teen America. Will Wes' parents help me financially? For that matter, will my parents help me? Should I get an abortion without telling my parents? Oh God, I don't know what to do!*

Another tear rolls down her cheek and it cascades over the knuckles on her hands folded in her lap. *Maybe I can keep the baby and have my very own little one who will love me and look to me for guidance. I can be a good mother. Sometimes I took care of Josie when she was a baby.* She stops crying at that thought.

I shouldn't have given into Wes, but I love him. Now he hates me for getting pregnant and ruining his future. Oh God, I'm scared. Please help me! Selah watches as the door of the building opens and a dozen girls pile out into the parking lot with their mothers. *Maybe I can stay at the girls' ranch and work until the baby comes. Then what?*

Josie is the last to emerge from the building as Selah wipes away her tears. She feigns a slight smile as Josie climbs in the front seat. Her little sister is full of smiles and verbosity as she expresses with enthusiasm, "Selah! I caught the baton today after throwing it up in the air!"

Selah is grateful that Josie hasn't noticed that her eyes are red from crying. "That's great, Stinkweed. It took a lot of practice, but you did it. Put on your seatbelt."

"Now, I have to learn to toss it high enough so I can spin while it's in the air," says Josie, ignoring Selah's request. "Do you think I should get my hair cut, or put it in a ponytail? My friend Mary gets hers cut short like her mom's. I'm gonna practice when we get home and show Mommy."

Selah allows Josie to ramble on about anything and everything. She isn't listening, and stares straight ahead without starting the ignition. She doesn't look over at her little sister for fear that Josie might see on her face that something is wrong.

Josie continues her one-sided conversation as the parking lot empties of people and cars. "Let's open all the windows! It's windy and it's gonna rain!" Josie looks over at the dragon on the island across the Indian River and spies the dark, swelling mass of swirling clouds. She listens to the rumbles of thunder as the storm approaches the mainland. "OOOH! A bad storm is coming! Let's go across the bridge so we can feel the wind lift up the car like it did that one day, remember?"

"We're not going across the bridge, we're going home," Selah responds as she starts the car. To change the subject before Josie can protest, Selah asks, "Are you spotting when you twirl like I showed you so that you can keep your balance?"

"Selah, I can't do twirls in place until I can toss the baton high enough and catch it. Duh!"

"OK, one thing at a time," they both say in unison.

"Dunderhead!" teases Josie.

"You're the dunderhead, Stinkweed!" banters Selah in response as she slows at the stop sign before a left turn onto Pineapple Avenue. She notices how the gusts of wind arising from the oncoming winter thunderstorm loosen the leaves of the trees, and blows them around and around in tiny tornadoes. She also sees Jane and Donna across the street in Pineapple Park next to the library, sitting on the swings and eating ice cream cones. *Humph. Jane: pale, short and overweight; Donna: dark, tall and slender; an unusual pair. What are* they *doing together?*

As she makes a left turn, Selah's attention is brought back to Josie, who still rambles on about her friend. All of a sudden, Josie flings violently sideways toward Selah. The baton soars in the air and smacks Selah in the head.

"Josie! What are you doing? Get up!" Selah demands as she looks down at her sister's head, which almost rests on her lap. Like an incoming tide, crimson blood spreads ever-widening onto Josie's face. As she watches with horror, Selah shrieks, "Josie!" Selah inadvertently presses down on the accelerator, takes her hands off of the steering wheel, and screams as the car rams headlong into the trunk of a large oak tree.

CHAPTER 17

"Did you see *The Passion of the Christ*?" Donna asks Jane as they exit the library with the books they have checked out.

"Yes, it was very bloody, violent…and sad," she responds with a note of finality. "I really don't want to think about it or I'll start crying all over again. Let's get some ice cream," she says when she spots the ice cream vendor's small truck in the parking lot.

As Jane directs her attention toward the truck full of frozen goodies, Donna continues to talk about the movie. "Just think though, the violence that was portrayed in the movie wasn't nearly as terrible as the actual beating that He endured before the cross. Jesus was beaten so badly that he couldn't even be recognized. And He didn't even do anything wrong to be punished for!"

"That's the reason a lot of people went to see the movie," Jane adds. "For the violence. A lot of them didn't even decide to join God's side after seeing what Jesus did for them."

"I like the way you put that – 'God's side,'" Donna says, with a misty look in her eyes. "But *some* people started reading the Bible after seeing the movie. They actually realized that they wanted whatever it was that Jesus thought was important enough to die for. How can anyone reject the gift that Jesus died to give to us? Shouldn't everyone feel so grateful to this man that they would want to 'join His side'? There's nothing on earth that compares with being born again and knowing what's in your future."

"Jared mentioned that phrase one night in my living room. What does it mean exactly, Donna? Are you saying that *you're* 'born again'?"

Donna smiles tenderly at her new friend as they sit upon the swings in the park. "I suppose the best way to define it is: it's a rebirth of who you are on the *inside;* there's a change that comes over you, a change from a hardened heart full of self-pride to a soft, patient heart with a loving attitude toward others and tremendous love for Jesus for taking *my* punishment! I know it sounds like a lot of mushiness that can't be real. That's why a lot of people turn away from the idea of being born again; it seems overstated and exaggerated religious fanaticism. It's very difficult to understand exactly what it means; even Jesus said that it's hard to understand; when He was trying to explain it to a well-educated Jewish leader, he told him that one must be born again to enter God's kingdom."[1] She hesitates a moment, deep in thought. "Let me see if I can remember the Scripture from my *Extreme Teen Bible.* 'The wind blows where it wants to and you can hear the sound of it, but you don't know where it comes from or where it's going. It's the same with everyone who is born of the Spirit. [1] That's just another expression for 'born again.'"

"Born of the Spirit? What is…'The Spirit?'

"God gives it to you when you believe in Jesus and what He did for you. He knows when you are ready to acquire this power. Keep asking Him for it until you receive it. You'll know when you *do* get it; it's like a light bulb going off in your head, and you start understanding the Scriptures and what Jesus taught. You also feel differently toward people who aren't saved or who once aggravated you, because you realize that they don't have what you have, and you want them to have it too because it's so incredible! That's why those who aren't saved and born again think that we believe that we are better than they are…" Donna looks directly at Jane and emphasizes her next statement. **"We aren't better than they are; we have something that they're missing,** because they don't *know* that they are lost and missing something very important in their lives! We have knowledge of the Bible's truth that unbelievers don't have, and **knowledge *is* power!**

"Things don't irritate me anymore because they aren't important compared to the knowledge I have, and I'm still learning! When you're filled with the Spirit, you're filled with indescribable happiness and peace… Those of us who have the Spirit realize that we have been born again. The Holy Spirit is God's way of letting us know that we are truly saved. If you're not *sure* that you are saved, then you *aren't.* In fact, I have a confession to make to you; that day that Selah pushed everything off of your lap on the last day of school last year, remember?"

Jane nods her head as Donna continues.

"For the rest of the day, I was upset about what had happened; all I could think about was how your feelings must have been hurt, and I felt guilty for not helping you that day. I followed Selah instead of staying to help you, and I sincerely apologize for that. I prayed that night to receive God's Spirit so that I could learn to be holy like Jesus.

"I know this is going to sound silly to you," Donna continues, "but when I was by myself in my room that night, I was born again; how exactly, I don't know; but I *do* know that it happened. Oh Jane, it's so unbelievable! Jesus is in my heart!"

Jane looks at Donna's face. Her eyes are sparkling! She looks so happy!

"Oh, Jane! There's so much more for you to learn about the Holy Spirit, but I don't want to overwhelm you! This is what was so important that Jesus sacrificed Himself for it, so that we all can have a chance to be right with God and be saved, by being grateful for what He did for us, and to receive His Spirit, and to have the gifts of the Spirit, and to manifest the 'fruit of the Spirit'…!"

Jane was amazed. "Whoa! Slow down! You really are excited about all this stuff, aren't you? Do you know that your ice cream has melted and is dripping off your elbow? There's a little puddle in the sand!" Jane grabs a napkin from her jeans pocket, which is bulging with them.

They both start laughing. Jane wipes away the stream of vanilla ice cream from Donna's milk chocolate skin. Then they hear a loud crash. Turning their attention toward the direction of the sound, they see a car with its hood crunched around a large oak tree. Jane recognizes the car and drops what is left of her ice cream cone. "It's Selah and Josie!" she screams as she runs toward the scene.

Donna also drops her cone, and follows after Jane.

Jane arrives and peers into the passenger side of the car, where she frantically deflates the air bag and sees Josie unconscious on the floor. Donna runs around to check on Selah, who is attempting to unbuckle herself from the seatbelt, but the airbag is hindering her efforts.

Shaking, Selah asks, "Where did all this blood come from? There was a tree and then…" Selah stops as if in shock. "What happened? Where's Josie? I can't get this off!"

Then, as though from a long distance away, Selah hears Jane scream the words, "Josie has a pulse but she's not breathing!" Selah grabs her forehead where the baton had smacked her violently when Josie had been flung sideways. She meekly utters, "No, Josie!"

Selah and Donna watch as Jane pulls Josie's limp body from the car, places her on the pavement, and begins to blow life into the little girl's lungs.

The torrential storm comes ashore. Giant drops of cold rain begin to pound them and the pavement. A blast of thunder echoes in Selah's head.

Donna pulls out her cell phone and dials 911. Jane begins her work on Josie. As she waits for someone to answer her ardent call for help, Donna falls to her knees and begins to silently pray.

Selah manages to free herself from the restraint of the seatbelt and stumbles her way around to the other side of the car. *I hurt so much. Where did all this blood on my lap come from?* "She's going to be alright, isn't she, Jane?" Selah sobs meekly. She sits down with her knees to her chest and hugs herself as she rocks back and forth.

"Here!" Jane orders Selah. "Take these napkins and hold them on Josie's head, right here, and press to stop the flow of blood!" Selah sits unmoving. "Selah! Do it!" Jane yells as she stuffs the napkins into Selah's hand.

Jane checks to see if Josie has begun to breathe. *Please don't die, Josie!* She repositions the child's head and continues her attempt at artificial respiration. *Help me do this right. Please, God!* Jane thinks silently to herself. *Breathe, breathe Josie!*

Suddenly, after what seemed like an hour, Jane sees Josie's chest rise on its own.

"Selah! She's breathing!" exclaims Jane.

They hear a siren as it rounds the corner onto Pineapple Avenue. The raindrops, hard as pearls, begin to pelt them with potent power. Another crash of thunder explodes overhead as the paramedics race over to the little girl who lies on the road. All at once, the full force of the storm erupts to expel its furious rage.

CHAPTER 18

In the emergency room an hour later, Selah awakes to see a nurse standing over her. "You had to have a D & C. Did you know that you were pregnant?" the plump nurse inquires with insensitivity as she moves some equipment out of the way. "You had a miscarriage. Your parents arrived while you were in surgery."

"Do they know?" Selah asks with some fear.

"No, they were only told that you were with the doctor."

"Where's my little sister? Is she all right?"

"I'll send in your mom and dad now," the nurse says with a slight smile on her round face. She quickly leaves the room.

Selah closes her eyes for a brief moment. The next thing she knows is that her parents are each holding one of her hands.

"Mom, Dad, how's Josie?"

"We don't know yet," John responds tenderly.

"They are doing an MRI right now," says Esther as she pats her daughter's hand. "How are you feeling? You have quite a bump on your head."

"Oh, yeah, from Josie's baton hitting me in the accident," explains Selah as she touches it lightly. "I'm sorry about the car, Dad. Everything happened so fast. Josie was bleeding from her head *before* we hit the tree."

Selah has an intense look of worry in her eyes. "What happened to her? Do the doctors know anything?"

"They said they'll know more after the MRI," John answers, "but did you say that Josie was injured *before* the accident?"

Selah nods, almost imperceptibly.

"Are you up to answering some questions that the police want for their report?" questions Esther. "There's an Officer Cord here, waiting to speak to you."

"Sure. I guess so. Can you stay with me? Both of you?"

"I'll let him know," says Esther. Then she turns around and leaves the room.

John squeezes Selah's hand and kisses her on the head, being careful not to touch the bump on her forehead, which is swollen and bruised.

"Don't worry about the car, Honey. I'm more worried about the two of *you*."

Selah gives her father a feeble smile as a policeman enters the room. Esther follows close behind him.

"Bill, this is my daughter Selah," John says. "Selah, this is Bill Cord. Bill and I went to high school together. The two of us were catching up with each other while you were being checked by Dr. Martinez."

Selah explains everything that she can recall about the incident with Josie's baton which led up to the accident. He takes a few notes and thanks Selah for the information. "I'll stay here awhile at the nurses' desk if you should need me, John."

"Thank you, Bill."

They shake hands and Officer Cord leaves the room.

"Well, that wasn't too bad, was it?" queries Esther with some nervousness. "I'm going to go out to the waiting room. By the way, you have some friends here."

"Would you like to see them now?" John questions. "Or do you want to rest?"

"I'm OK, Daddy. They can come in. I want to thank Jane for saving Josie's life. Please let me know the minute you hear anything about Josie, promise?" She glances back and forth between her parents at her request to be kept informed.

"Of course we will; as soon as we know anything," Esther replies.

Her father gives her a big smile and another squeeze of her hand before he walks away from her bedside.

John is out of the door, but Esther returns to Selah and gently gives her daughter a kiss on the cheek. Selah is taken aback because she can't remember when her mother has ever kissed her before. She has received kisses from her father, but not from her mother. After Esther expresses love to her daughter, she quickly runs out of the room.

Jane and Donna now enter and stand together on one side of the bed. No one speaks immediately, but all three girls smile at each other.

"What are you wearing?" asks Selah with amusement on her face.

Jane smiles shyly and looks up at Donna. Donna replies, "Our clothes were soaked, so the nurse let us change into these clean scrubs. My pants are a little short and Jane's are way too long for her. How's your head feel? There's quite a large bulge there."

"I'm OK; I just want to find out about Josie and what happened to her."

While the girls converse, Paul, Faith, Simon and Jared Preston join John and Esther in the waiting room. Simon and Faith hug like old friends, which surprises Paul. "I had no idea that you two knew each other."

Faith says, "I attend his church now. He convinced me of the truth about Sabbath. I want to sincerely thank you, Simon, for talking to Paul and explaining Jesus' message to him, and more truth to me, also. I missed him very much while he was gone," she says as she smiles tenderly at her husband. Jared and Faith hug each other as they greet.

"Where's Josie?" inquires Jared.

"She's still in the MRI room," responds Faith. "The doctor said it would take about an hour and it's been longer than that, so I'm sure we'll hear something sometime soon."

Outside the storm has abated, but the sky is laden with heavy, gray clouds. Daniel, David, and Adam return to Daniel's house and turn on the television. The three of them turn their attention to the TV screen when they hear a report about a car accident on Pineapple Avenue. "The mayor of Rocky Water, John Abrams, was called away from his office this afternoon. Approximately two hours ago, the mayor was informed that his two daughters had been involved in a one-car accident. Both girls are currently being treated by Dr. Juan Martinez at Harbor City Hospital. Our reporter is en route to the hospital now and will update us on the two girls as soon as their conditions are known. And now to national news…"

Daniel and Adam look over at David, who seems to be in a slight state of shock. "Leave your car here, David," says Daniel. "I'll drive us to the hospital." *Please let Selah be all right!* Daniel pleads silently.

Twenty minutes later, the three boys walk into the emergency room, over to where the others are still awaiting news of the results of Josie's test. Ten silent minutes go by, and then Dr. Martinez slowly walks into the room with his arms folded across his chest. He grips a folder of papers. Everyone notices the dismal look of uncertainty on his face. John stands to his feet.

"She's holding her own," he explains quickly, with uplifted hands to calm down the family before they can panic. "She's conscious. I apologize for the long wait you all had to endure, but I was consulting with another doctor for her opinion about the results of the MRI. Something bounced off of her temple area and caused a skull fracture. We see no shards of glass, which we would normally expect to find from a car accident. And..." he hesitates before his next words, "Her neck is critically injured. She has no feeling in her arms or legs."

"Oh no!" Esther gasps as she places her hands over her mouth.

John sits down and puts his arm around his wife. He leans forward with his head in his other hand. No one else in the room moves or makes a sound.

Jane and Donna return from Selah's room and stand in the doorway. They have heard the last sentence that the doctor had spoken.

"She's paralyzed?" Jane reiterates to make sure that she has heard correctly.

Dr. Martinez turns around and faces the girls in the doorway, then turns back around to speak to John. "I have here in this folder some forms that need to be signed. I'll go over each form with you. I recommend that exploratory surgery be done. I've contacted the neurosurgeon."

Donna and Jane enter the waiting room and sit next to Adam and David. Jane sees that Daniel is standing in the corner of the room, away from the others. His head is hung low and his arms are folded tightly across his chest. She thinks she sees a tear roll down his cheek.

Jared gets up from his seat and sits down next to Adam. They each stare at the other for a moment, but say nothing to each other.

"Of course I'll sign the forms," John answers the doctor with certainty. He removes his arm from around Esther and stands. Esther leans forward and places her head in her hands in complete despair.

"While I sign these forms..." says John, "Esther? Are you up to telling Selah what's going on? We promised that we would inform her as soon as we got any news about Josie." John waits for Esther to lift her head and answer him.

"Yes, all right. I'll tell her." The next thing out of her mouth shocks David. "David? Would you like to come with me?"

He is stunned for a second and then says, "Sure, if you'd like me to."

John and Dr. Martinez retreat from the waiting area and enter the doctor's office.

Esther slowly rises from her seat and David follows her into Selah's room.

"Mom," Selah responds. "How's Josie? Hey, David, I'm glad that you're here. Is there any news yet?" It's then that Selah becomes aware of the serious looks on their faces.

"Josie has a skull fracture. She can't move her arms and legs," answers Esther.

Not much consideration for Selah's already weakened condition, thinks David. He observes the fearful concern come over his cousin's face as she absorbs the news.

Then after a moment of contemplation, Selah remembers the blood *before* the accident. "What happened to cause her head to bleed before the car hit the tree? I don't understand any of this. She hit me in the head with her baton, and I lost control of the car. Her body fell over and she was almost in my lap; that's when I saw a lot of blood in her hair and I freaked out."

David is now full of confusion and concern over the words he hears.

"Are you sure, Selah? She was hurt *before* the car hit the tree?" queries Esther.

"Yes, I'm positive. Her head was bleeding *before* we crashed into the tree."

David's head feels like it will burst open from the pressure within. His heart pounds out of control and his head burns with such searing pain that he can't seem to remain steady on his feet. *Can this be true? Is it what I think it is? Oh, God, please don't let it be true! We were at Dragon Point at 3:30; Josie leaves her lessons at 3:30....* David stumbles over to the chair next to the bed and sits down before he falls down in a dead faint. Only one thought races through his mind; only one image of himself, firing the bullet that went astray. He leans forward and puts his head between his knees to overcome the sensation that he will pass out. He's never felt faint before in his life.

Selah is stupefied at what her mother does next.

"David! What is it? Are you all right?" Esther inquires, as she hurries over to touch the back of David's head with affection. She gasps at the large bump she feels.

This is the second time today that mom is doing something that I've never seen her do before! She's actually showing real concern for David!

David's heart fills with overflowing dread at the possibility that what he thinks may have happened is actually true. He hears his Aunt Esther speaking to him, but he can't make out what she's saying. Her words are a just a jumbled stack of syllables when they reach his brain.

Esther kneels down beside David. "David! Look at me! Can you hear me? You've been hurt! You might have a concussion. I'm getting a nurse in here to check on you." Esther turns and bustles out the door.

"David! What's wrong?" Selah asks after her mother leaves. She sits up too quickly and becomes lightheaded, so she lies down again. David lifts his head to confront her with his confession.

"Selah, I…I…" There are tears in his eyes.

"It's all right, David. Tell me," encourages Selah with love and tenderness in her voice.

Barely audible, David stutters, "I, I think I sh…shot…Josie."

CHAPTER 19

"What did you say? I can't understand what you're telling me, David."

"I did this to Josie. My stupid, arrogant pride did this to her. *I shot her!*"

After holding her breath and with a heart full of fear, she lets out a mournful gasp. She places her hands over her mouth as tears well up in her eyes. She rolls over onto her side and slowly sits up in order to be closer to David. As she does so, she is able to see her friends standing in the doorway. By the look on their faces, she surmises that they have overheard David's confession.

The group of friends is filled with numb panic. Slowly, one by one, they make their way into the room, except for Adam; he stands frozen in place. Daniel and Jared go to David, who has his elbows on his knees with his head in his hands. Jane and Donna walk slowly to Selah's bedside, where they had been just moments before.

With minds benumbed and mouths agape, no one is able to utter a word. After a few moments of silence, Donna dissolves the solemn reticence. "Jared, come with me," she orders with an air of authority. Jared follows.

They leave and Esther and the plump nurse enter Selah's room. "*This boy, right here,*" Esther says to the nurse as she points to David in the chair.

The nurse parts David's hair and she examines the large bump. "Hm. That needs to be looked at, young man. Follow me into the exam room." David rises from his seated position and shuffles slowly behind the nurse.

Donna and Jared join Paul and Faith, where they sit in the waiting room with Simon. The third-floor room is empty except for the five of them.

"I think that we should go see Josie," Donna informs the others.

Her father Simon has the same idea. "I agree. With our unity of faith, God will grant our prayer to heal Josie."

Jared heaves a deep sigh.

"Jared?" asks Simon with an inquisitive look. "Will you be joining us?"

"Maybe it's better if I stay with the others; not that I don't want to pray for Josie, but I think I should be with Adam and David."

The others nod their heads with silent understanding and leave the room.

Jared returns to Selah's room to find Adam sitting in the chair with his head down, elbows on his knees and hands clasped as if in prayer.

Adam is thinking, *why didn't I try to stop David from firing the gun? I just stood there and did nothing to prevent this. I had no control! Now someone else I love is going to die. God, I hate you!*

David rejoins his friends, holding a bag of ice to the back of his head.

Adam raises his eyes to gaze at David. No one expresses their thoughts for the moment.

Then David asks his friends, "What should I do? Should I tell someone?" *God, why did you let this happen? I* hate *you!* His eyes begin to burn and fill with tears.

The group is silent until Daniel replies with a courageous answer. "Yes, I think we should. I'll go with you to tell the police what we did. I'm just as guilty as you are, David. I knew it was wrong to steal my dad's gun." *I'm so stupid! I was trying to show off by being "The Big Man" in front of David and Adam.*

Adam rolls his eyes with disbelief at what he's hearing. "You're gonna turn yourselves in; confess to something that wasn't intentional? Why? You're crazy if you do. The gun will never be found in that lagoon. When Mr. Windfeather discovers it missing, he'll report it as stolen. Case closed!"

Selah and Jane look at the boys with admiration, but both are fearful for them for what may ensue if it goes to court. Daniel sees the sentiment in Selah's eyes. She looks at him in a way that he's never seen before.

David thinks, *I'll have a criminal record, but I have to turn myself in. Look at what I've done to Josie. She'll be in a wheelchair for the rest of her life!*

After Adam's statement, silence lingers in the air. Paul and Faith come into the room, holding hands. Simon and Donna follow close behind. Paul walks over to Adam who now stands up from the chair and allows his dad to put his arm around him.

"When I left the house," says Faith as she walks to Jane, "God's Holy Spirit told me to bring this along." In her hand is Stephen's notebook. "Here, Jane," she says as she extends it to her daughter.

Jane lowers her head and swallows deeply with helplessness. She takes the notebook from her mother.

"Doctor Martinez said that he has to call in a neurosurgeon to examine Josie," explains Paul. "How 'bout we go to the cafeteria and get some dinner while we wait for the neurosurgeon to arrive? Josie is sleeping now anyway."

All agree they are hungry except David, Daniel and Jared.

Selah says with a downcast countenance, "Go ahead. I'm not hungry."

The three boys wander into the waiting room as the others head toward the cafeteria.

The waiting area is empty and quiet. The television is not on, for which Jared is thankful. He glances around at the watercolor paintings on the pastel blue walls. Dark blue upholstered chairs are neatly arranged into cozy separate seating areas atop wall-to-wall carpet which has a tropical print.

Daniel and Jared sit down facing the windows.

David walks over to the large windows along the far wall and sees the vast expanse of dismal gray clouds that reflects his melancholy mood. *How can I be so mad at someone I can't see or reason with?* he thinks as he crosses his arms over his chest. *I don't think you can hear me or understand how I feel!* He screams with an inward silence.

Fighting the urge to cry, David lifts his chin in defiance of his tears. His misty eyes stare at the sky through rain-splattered window panes. He gazes with glum blankness at the tallest palm tree across the street as it sways gracefully in the flurries of wind. *If you really are the all-powerful God that Jared says you are, then do something!* David pleads as he leans his head against the window pane.

"I'm gonna go to the vending machine in the hall and get us some Cokes," says Daniel.

After Daniel leaves, Jared turns to David.

David can fight no longer. He falls to his knees and begins to sob with the tortuous pain in his heart.

Jared quietly states, "Give all of your pain to Jesus, David. He's been patiently waiting for you to invite Him into your life to help you with anything you ask of Him, but you must make the first move."

David turns his tear-sogged eyes up to Jared, who bends down to be face-to-face.

Jared can't perceive what is in David's mind at this critical juncture. *Is he going to turn away in anger because of his hate for You? Am I being too pushy, Lord? Is it the right time for me to ask if he's ready to take the first step? Give me the right words. Please, Lord.*

"Why is God so harsh? What does He *want* from me?!" David abruptly blurts out.

Jared speaks slowly and lovingly. "He wants you to learn from Him, to lean on Him in every circumstance that comes along in your life. He wants you… 'To act justly, be kind and merciful, and to walk humbly with Him.'[1] "He wants you to receive the gift of salvation that He's been waiting for you to ask Him for, the gift that Jesus died to make available to you. Please, David. Won't you take it now to end the suffering and emptiness you feel inside?"

David looks directly into Jared's eyes, where he sees pleading sadness.

Unknown to the two of them, Daniel opens the door to the waiting room and observes the unraveling scene. He's not sure what to do, so he stands frozen in place as he hears David repeat the words that solemnly flow forth from Jared's mouth. Daniel steps quietly backwards out of the door as David and Jared pray together.

"Father God, I ask you to forgive my sins and disobedience to your loving kindness. I know Jesus is the savior of my soul. He died to give me a choice to accept the gift of eternal life with you. I believe that his resurrection is an example of what you'll do for me because I take your gift of salvation through faith in your amazing grace. In Jesus' name I pray, Amen."

Silence lingers in the air between the two boys. They both have tears in their eyes. Then, the most amazing thing happens. The sun is low in the sky. A brilliant, narrow beam of sunlight breaks through the clouds and falls on the two of them. The light casts a shadow across the carpet to the door where Daniel had stood a moment ago. They both avert their eyes from the sudden brightness of the sunlight and observe their shadows on the door.

Jared hears a calm quiet voice within himself whisper, "Tell him…." Jared listens, turns to David and conveys, "You are now forgiven of all misdeeds against God. He takes your guilt and shame upon himself. You no longer have anything of which you are guilty. You are saved and free from the results of sin."

David stares blankly at their shadows on the door, unmoving and void of any expression of acknowledgement that he has heard Jared's message.

Jared turns his eyes to squint into the sunlight from where he sits on the floor next to David. He doesn't see David turn to gaze at him.

Suddenly, another amazing thing happens. David notices a look of enthrallment come to Jared's face. Jared reaches out to touch David's arm as he continues to stare up at the sky. David turns to peer out the window.

With wide-eyed wonder, he is awestruck at what he sees. On the ledge outside is a tall, white American egret, the largest one David has ever seen. The slender bird doesn't flinch as it stands on delicate legs and extends its long elegant neck.

Jared and David sit frozen in place as the egret slowly walks the length of the ledge in their direction. When it reaches them, it stops and slants its head down to peer at them.

David slowly and carefully rises to his knees, full of wonderment at what is happening. He expects the bird to fly away, but instead it tilts its head, lifts one leg slightly off the ledge, and peers directly into David's eyes. Only an inch from the window pane, boy and bird are captivated with one another.

Jared is mesmerized, unable to move as he witnesses this almost inconceivable occurrence unfolding in front of him. Softly, with punctuated exactness and a pause between each word, Jared whispers, "This is unbelievable!"

David responds with a slight smile on his lips and a peaceful brightness in his eyes. The egret blinks its eyes and gradually lowers its limb to once again stand on both legs. David warily and slowly lifts his hand and hopes that he doesn't scare away the timid fowl. The elegant bird tilts its head downward and follows the movement of David's index finger as he touches the glass near the head of the feathered creature.

Once again, the egret meets David's awe-filled gaze in a moment of mutual fascination. He watches as the splendid white creature spreads its wings, steps off of the ledge, and flies upward in the midst of the single ray of sunlight.

David squints against the brightness of the radiating beam. He can scarcely believe the peace he feels within himself now. *Where did this sense of peace come from all of a sudden?* Then a soft tranquil voice says into his ear, "Josie will be OK. Come to me now before it's too late."[2] This startles him, but he says nothing to Jared.

Jared rises to his knees to be next to his new friend. They both keep their eyes on the flight of the great American egret until it ascends out of sight.

CHAPTER 20

Meanwhile, in the hospital cafeteria, Adam has finished his dinner. As the others linger over dessert, he says something out of character, which shows his concern for Josie. It almost seems as though he is thinking out loud. "I wish that I had Harry Potter's magical powers, so that I could cast a spell to make Josie better."

Everyone looks at him, but no one knows what to say. Silence unnerves Adam at the moment, so he continues to express his thoughts aloud, not with compassion as in his first wishful statement, but with irritable confusion in his voice.

"How could God let this happen? There's so many 'bad things that happen to good people.' It's not fair that I don't have more control. I want to have special knowledge and secret powers of magic and wizardry so that I can make everything the way that *I* want them to be. All my hard work studying in school…if I can't learn how to control things, what good does it do for me to learn all that nonsense?"

Simon feels compelled to answer. "Adam, I agree with you about wanting to have more control. If you hadn't been taught all the basic knowledge in school, you would not be able to understand that there's secret knowledge 'at your fingertips' that you *can* obtain in order to have more power *and* control. Actually, the knowledge is available to anyone who will seek it."

Simon continues, permeating the contemplative silence at the table. "Sure, those *Harry Potter* books are fun to read, and magic is fun, but let me tell you, Harry disregards rules and hopes that he doesn't get caught. He makes it appear as though witchcraft were interesting and desirable to learn; but, if we invite supernatural forces of this occult practice to bring harm to good people, it's not wise to tolerate them."[1]

"Magic in all ages has always represented a deep, unholy distortion of the divinely ordained relationships between creature, Creation and Creator. God's instructions to people in Leviticus 19:31 says, 'Do not turn to mediums or seek out spiritists, for you will be defiled by them. I am the Lord your God'. In other words, God wants you to turn to Him, and He will use you to exert His power to control things according to *His* will. Turn all control over to God; leave everything in His hands. It's through prayer and listening to the Holy Spirit within us that we can utilize God's power. What you want isn't magic or the ability to cast spells, but to have the Holy Spirit within you, so you can ask God to use His power through you in all that happens in life. The Holy Spirit also helps you to discern between what's *truth* and what's a lie, but you must first acquire the Holy Spirit by asking for it. God is very powerful. Don't underestimate what He is able to do."

Jane suddenly expresses a thought. "Is that why Stephen titled his notebook, 'Children Walking in Truth'?"

"I believe that he got that phrase from the third book of John, verse four," Simon adds.

Adam doesn't want to hear any more of this, so he changes the subject. "When is that doctor gonna get here and work on Josie?"

Paul replies, "Dr. Martinez said that he'll notify us when the neurosurgeon is prepared to speak with us. He knows that we're here in the cafeteria."

"Hey y'all, listen to what Stephen wrote here," says Jane.

"'What is the single most important characteristic of God? Some would answer that it's His power; others would say that it's His holiness. But God wants us to know that it is His *glory* which is His most important characteristic. In Exodus 33, Moses asks God to show him His glory. Glory could be translated "heavy weight," the biggest, grandest characteristic of someone, the sum total of their worth. (Webster's Dictionary) God's response to Moses is:

'I will pass by you with all of my goodness but you cannot see my face, for no one can see me and live.'(Exodus 33:19, 20). 'I am the Lord, full of mercy and patience and grace. I have deep love for thousands of people, forgiving wickedness, rebellion and sin. But I will not allow the sins of the wicked to go unpunished.' (Exodus 34:6, 7). Jesus said to follow Him and His ways, to give up our sinful ways and thoughts, to be born again of the Spirit in order to be renewed and saved from destruction.'"

Then Jane's eyes fill with horror at what she sees written on the opposite page from where she has just read aloud to everyone. No one at the table notices.

While the group discusses deep issues over their dessert in the cafeteria, the neurosurgeon examines the new set of MRI scans he had ordered done upon his arrival. "I don't understand," he says to the plump nurse. "Martha, I was told that this child had a skull fracture and a critical neck injury. I don't see that in these MRIs. Are you sure that these are Josephine Abrams' X-rays?"

"Yes, I'm positive, Dr. Chambers. I followed through the entire procedure and hand-carried them to you myself."

"This is quite strange," responds Dr. Chambers. "Where's her room? I want to examine her myself."

All at once, Martha grabs the doctor's arm and begins shaking it with such excitement that her mouth is wide open. "Dr. Chambers! This is a case of miraculous healing! It must be! This is a first in all of my twenty-seven years of nursing!" Martha cups her hands over her mouth and her jaw drops. Then she raises her arms in the air with wide open hands, turns away from the doctor, and begins prancing around the small room.

With a baffled look on his face, Dr. Chambers watches the silly, childish dance of a mature adult. "Woman! Have you gone insane? Fetch the family to my office ASAP." He shakes his head with hilarious disbelief, places the film in the folder and leaves the room.

Dr. Chambers finds Josie dozing in bed, and he decides to perform a test. He takes out a sharp needle, lifts the sheets to uncover the child's feet, and gently pokes the bottom of Josie's right foot.

Her head turns quickly as her leg draws abruptly away from the source of pain. "OW! Hey, I felt that!" Josie says in confusion, wondering what just woke her up. "I can move my arms and legs now. Are you the doctor who fixed me? My neck still hurts though."

The doctor shakes himself out of his stupor of non-belief. "Let me take a gander at the back of that sore neck of yours," he requests as he walks around to the head of the bed. He examines her neck. "It's going to be sore for a while. The vertebrae in your neck took the full brunt of the impact with the gear shift in the accident. You have quite a bad bruise there. I'll have the nurse rub some vinegar on it for you, OK?"

Josie gazes with a warm smile at the tall, elderly doctor who she thinks fixed her arms and legs. His warm grey eyes have many wrinkles around the outside corners, she notices. She also takes note that he stands in place and rubs his chin and then the back of his neck with a look of bewilderment behind those grey eyes. *I thought that he said he was going to get the nurse to come in here.* "I'm Josie. What's your name?"

"Hm? Oh, I'm Dr. Chambers," he replies in a befuddled manner. "I'll go get Nurse Martha and send her in here with some vinegar for that bruise, all right, young lady? You stay in bed for now, understood?"

Josie gives him a huge smile in return. "OK, Dr. Chambers."

He runs into the nurse in the hallway and gives her his orders for Josie's treatment.

"The family is in your office now, doctor," she tells him.

"Thank you, Martha. I'm on my way now." *How do I explain this to them?* he wonders as he walks down the hall. He smacks himself in the forehead with the palm of his hand. *"What's wrong with me? This is good news! Though, I don't understand how this happened. I saw the first set of X-rays, and there was extensive damage to her neck!* He smiles to himself as he walks down the hall. *This is good news indeed!* When he reaches his office door he takes a deep breath, and stands for a moment to stare at the large brown envelope. He lets out his breath and opens the door.

After he closes the door behind him, he looks at each of their faces, some swollen from crying, and the rest burdened with worry. He scratches his head and walks around to the other side of his desk. "Um…hello. I'm Dr. Chambers," he utters as he plops down in his extravagant leather chair behind the huge desk. "I can't explain it, but…" he speaks slowly, fighting to find the right words. He suddenly leans forward and opens the folder still in his hand and pulls out the MRI. The other large folder on his desk contains the first MRIs, taken when Josie was brought into the emergency room over four hours ago. From this he removes the photo and he lays it next to the X-ray taken just thirty minutes ago.

"When I arrived, I ordered another X-ray of Josephine's head and neck. This one here," he says as he points to the first one, "was taken when she was first brought in. You can see the damage to her vertebrae, but… this one was taken less than an hour ago."

Everyone now stands and peers down at the photos. They don't fully comprehend what they are seeing, but they clearly observe the difference between the two.

While glancing back and forth between John and Esther, Dr. Chambers throws up his hands in the air and raises his eyebrows, seemingly speechless.

Suddenly, Donna's mouth falls open and ecstasy fills her eyes. "Daddy! Our prayer has been answered!"

"It most certainly has, honey!" Simon exclaims with a large grin on his face.

Esther and John look at each other with stunned amazement. "What? What did you say?" Esther can't believe her ears.

Jane, Paul and Faith, eyes wide with awe and wonderment, gaze into each other's faces.

Then to assure that he understands what Dr. Chambers attempts to convey, John mumbles with hesitancy, "You mean that…that… she's no longer paralyzed? She's going to be all right?" he asks with stark disbelief at this amazing turn of events.

"I can't explain it medically, but yes, that's what I'm telling you," replies Dr. Chambers. "She's been completely restored to health. Her neck and skull have somehow been healed." [2]

The room bursts with joy, laughter, and hugs. Faith even embraces Dr. Chambers, whose face is stunned at the show of affection from this stranger. Jane follows her mother's lead and does the same.

Josephine is obviously much loved, he thinks silently. This time, the doctor is ready for the family's attack of happiness and gratitude directed at him, as though *he* were the one who had miraculously healed the little girl.

CHAPTER 21

"I'd like to keep both girls overnight for observation," Dr. Martinez informs all in Dr. Chambers' office. "You may see Josie briefly now, and you may stay with Selah until visiting hours are over tonight. You can check them out tomorrow about noon after my hospital rounds, all right?"

John shakes the doctor's hand and thanks him for taking such good care of his daughters.

After visiting Josie for a few minutes, they all leave quietly when she falls asleep.

Jane jogs to Selah's room. She sees Selah sitting up in bed. Daniel is already there. As she walks in, she notices that Daniel and Selah quickly let go of each other's hands at her sudden appearance. Jane pretends that she hasn't seen the mutual show of affection between them.

"Selah! Daniel! Josie is all right. She's going to be OK, back to her normal self! Where are David and Jared? I have to tell them too! Are they in the waiting room? I'll go look!" Jane spins around to exit just as the others arrive in the doorway. Selah and Daniel are speechless, but full of smiles as the others come in. Daniel stands up and offers the chair to Donna.

In the waiting room, Jane finds Jared and David sitting next to each other, conversing quietly. They are the only ones in the room. It is now dark outside, but the overhead lights illuminate the two boys.

"Guys! Josie is healed! Can you believe it? Her neck was broken, but now it's all right! She's back to normal, squirming all over the place!" Jane is so beside herself that she doesn't realize that her behavior seems erratic to the two boys. They stand up when she enters.

"David! Isn't it wonderful?" she asks as she jumps up to hug his neck. He returns the hug and then she realizes what she has done. She meekly lets go of him and gives him a shy smile.

He is weak with gratitude that his little cousin will be all right; so much so that he falls to his knees. He begins to laugh out of control with relief, but he doesn't care. *Josie is OK!* David looks up at Jared with a deep smile in his eyes. Jared returns the look of affection and gratefulness to their unseen God for what He has done. Jared bends down and helps David rise to his feet.

Jane senses that Josie's healing isn't the only miracle that has happened in the hospital tonight. "You both go ahead and visit Selah," instructs Jane with a shy smile. "I just want to be alone for a few minutes. I'll join y'all later."

"OK, Jane," Jared replies with a tender squeeze to her forearm.

She sits down in the chair that David had vacated and opens the notebook. She once again reads the words that had sent shivers down her spine in the cafeteria:

'Saul Evans burst into our meeting tonight...'

He's the boy who killed Stephen! She fills with hatred at the sight of his name.

'His face was red with anger; fury was in his eyes toward all of us. I finally got him calmed down enough to sit down and listen, but only after he ranted and screamed to vent his rage. He doesn't agree with me and those who have discovered the truth. We meet in my dorm room to discuss the best way to relay the message of the most important news of anyone's life! It's hard for me to accept the fact that not very many people will...'

Jane hears the door open and watches David as he walks toward her.

"I know you said that you wanted to be alone, but I want to make sure that you're OK. May I join you?"

Jane slightly nods her head with surprise at the interruption, but smiles and pats the chair next to her, an invitation for David to sit down.

"Something is bothering you, Jane. I can see it in your face. Is it something in the notebook?"

Jane bends forward and places her head in her hands. She lets out a long sigh before raising her eyes to meet David's. "You and Stephen were close friends. We all grew up together. I loved my brother with all my heart, and when he was murdered..." She lets her voice trail off into silence.

"I know that I was..." David begins but doesn't seem to know how to relay his thoughts either. "I was so angry at God for letting my parents die; and then when Stephen died less than two years after that, I thought that I was going to lose my mind. I didn't want to live. I often thought about suicide, but I couldn't do that to Josie, to have her hate me for leaving her because I was thinking only of myself. I was almost there, Jane, ready to end my life right there in my room, and Josie burst in and gave me a hug. I had forgotten to lock the door!" he admits with a silly grin. "I'll never forget how I felt that evening when she jumped up on my bed to be next to me. She wanted to read to me her favorite book, *Little Lost Angel.*[1] Do you remember that the story starts on the night that Jesus was born and how this young angel helps a lot of people?"

Jane nods her head. "Yes, I remember it. Christmastime, like now. It's only four days away. But Jesus is *not* a little baby in a manger anymore. We know that better than most people, don't we?" She smiles a knowing smile, because David saw Him too that night in her dining room.

"I want to show you what Stephen wrote about the boy who killed him," she says.

"What?" interrupts David with a disturbed look in his eyes. "Stephen knew him before that night? The police thought that it was just another random shooting by a crazed gunman on the warpath."

She reads to David up to where she left off when he had come into the waiting room and then continues on:

"'It's hard for me to accept the fact that not very many people will be saved and go to heaven. If only everyone would listen and not close their eyes and ears to the truth in the Bible's message. Those words are from God Himself! How could anyone turn away without learning how to stop sinning and be able to live forever?! There are so many mysteries and fantastic secrets that He wants us to know if only we would spend as much time reading the Bible as we do playing computer games!

Saul Evans is a computer genius. He enjoys opening up porn sites with his girlfriend until I told them that they were sinning against God. The Holy Spirit filled my friend Linda and helped her to fight the sinful lust that she had once had! The Holy Spirit can help anyone who finds the secret to acquiring Him! Linda can't believe it. She never thought that her life could be turned completely around! But Saul is very angry that Linda has stopped having sex with him. She hadn't known before that it is sin in God's eyes to have pre-marital relations."

I tried to talk to Saul about Linda's conversion, to tell him that she still loved him, and wanted to be his girlfriend. Linda and I want desperately for Saul to listen about Jesus, but he is so full of pride. Like the others who have joined the Bible lessons in my dorm, I'm trying to help him…"

Jane stops reading and closes the notebook. "David! Stephen was trying to help that boy, but he wouldn't listen. He was so filled with rage and hatred! He never gave himself the chance to hear and follow the truth that Stephen tried to explain to him. It's so sad that he died committing a sinful act: suicide."

After silent contemplation, Jane's heart fills with pity for the boy who killed Stephen. "I think that I'm able to forgive Saul Evans for killing my brother. Remember, Mr. Potiphar was filled with a spirit of murder, in that he was obsessed about gory movies and he made us do that absurd assignment? Maybe that's what happened to Saul."

David nods slowly as he recalls the bizarre "assignment" to plot the perfect murder. "Ya know what I think?" he says to Jane. "I learned this afternoon from Jared that forgiveness is the first step in getting closer to God and being saved. I want to stop hating the boy who killed Stephen, but I can't yet. And I'm still mad at God for taking my parents. Jared says that forgiveness comes with the help of the Holy Spirit inside of you when you're born again. You must have the Spirit already! How?"

Jane thinks for a moment. "I said the prayer of salvation about a week ago with my mom, soon after that ghost appeared in my house. She said that it's the first step in the right direction on the right path, and that it will take some effort to stay on the path and not get detoured along the way."

"Your mom is great," David comments tenderly. "I wish Aunt Esther would…"

Just then the door opens and the person who walks in causes a sudden stir of fear within the both of them. Jane is aghast. David stands up to confront him.

"Mr. Potiphar! What are *you* doin' here?"

"Please forgive me if I'm intruding," he replies with sincerity in his voice. "I heard about what happened to Selah, and I wanted to see how she was. I just came from her room. Jane, it took some convincing on my part, but your father agreed to let me come and apologize to the both of you after apologizing to all of them for my behavior. I know now what happened to me, and I'm never going to delve into that kind of evil again, believe me. I hope that I can forgive myself for involving you kids in my ignorant fascination with the occult. Will you forgive me?"

David looks down at the floor and sighs. Jane, however, stands up and says, "I forgive you."

David raises his head with uncertainty to gaze into the man's distraught face. He holds out his hand to Mr. Potiphar and they shake hands. David doesn't say anything, but the meaning is inferred by Mr. Potiphar. He smiles, turns around and walks slowly out the door.

Jane sits back down and she looks at the words her brother has left behind for her to discover.

David remains standing for a second, then sits down also. He is silent as he watches her read.

Suddenly, she looks up from the notebook. David peruses the depth of Jane's brown eyes and he realizes that something astounding has been revealed to her.

Jane grabs David's hand and says, "C'mon! The others have to hear this, too!"

The two of them rush into Selah's room, where there is laughter all around her bedside. Paul asks, "Did Mr. Potiphar talk to you?"

"Yes, Daddy, but I have something that I would like everyone to hear. Since I was Josie's age, I have wondered why, if Sunday is the seventh day, the Sabbath, why is it listed as the first day of the week on the calendar? Listen to what Stephen wrote:

'This is from *The Almost Forgotten Day* by Mark Finley:'[2] "'… scores of people in Christian churches are…defending a doctrine that has slipped into the church through tradition—a doctrine that is a myth and not a commandment of God. Jesus never gave any special endorsement to the first day of the week." (p 140). Sunday is the first day of the week, not Monday!'"

She forges ahead, reading aloud what Stephen has written. Simon and Faith simply smile at each other because they already know the truth about the Sabbath.

"'[Jesus] never sanctioned any change in His law or said one word about the first day of the week replacing the Holy Sabbath...the New testament is absolutely silent on the change of the Sabbath from Saturday to Sunday in honor of the resurrection.'" (p 141). "'*Baptism* is a memorial of His resurrection.'"[3] (p 140, italics added)

"'We were therefore buried with Him through baptism unto death in order that, just as Christ was raised from the dead through the glory of the Father, we too may live a new life. If we have been united with him like this in his death, we will certainly also be united with him in his resurrection.' (Romans 6:4, 5 NIV; Ibid, p 140)."[2]

"So," continues Jane as she reads from the notebook, "that means that because he was resurrected on a Sunday, it was mistakenly made the Sabbath in honor of Jesus being raised from the dead. 'Myths are easily accepted as truth if they have been around a long time.'" (p 11)

Jared adds, "And Satan has been around a long time to make sure that the truth is hidden and difficult to hear if one doesn't want to yield to God's authority. He is the highest authority, to which any one of us will have to answer on Judgment Day.'"

Adam becomes exasperated and lets out a long sigh of spurning skepticism. "That's just a load of brainwashing gibberish. Jesus was just a man who lived two thousand years ago! Who cares? *I* don't! And if there *is* a God, where is He? Huh?"

David responds, "Adam, don't you realize that Josie has just been miraculously healed? Who do you think did that? And have you forgotten what happened in your house that night? Who else could that have been but Jesus?!"

Adam stands, full of pride and rage. "Has everyone here gone over the deep end with this freakish Jesus fanaticism? Who cares what Jesus taught or when the Sabbath is anyway?" He frowns at all of them, then spins around and walks toward the door.

"Adam!" Jane pleads. "The fourth commandment is the *only* one that begins with the word *remember.* 'Remember the Sabbath, to keep it holy...'! You promised to keep the eighth commandment. Breaking or ignoring even *one* commandment is sinful from God's viewpoint—it's as if you have broken all if you break one." ³

Adam stops in place, but he doesn't even turn around to acknowledge Jane's plea to listen. He simply shakes his head and exits the room, leaving everyone in dismay.

Where only minutes ago there was laughter, there is now sadness for Adam's rebellious anguish—anguish due to his refusal and inability to hear the truth because his heart is dense and impenetrable, deceived by the ruler of this world, the prince of the power of the air whose spirit works in those who are disobedient to God.⁴

Jane moves to follow after her brother, but David grabs her arm to stop her. "Give him a minute Jane, then I'll talk to him, OK?"

Jane nods her head solemnly. "All right, David. I just think that..." Jane begins slowly, almost apologetically for her outburst of insistence toward her brother. "I think that we need to uncover every truth that God has for us to discover, even that Christmas, Easter and Halloween are traditions that He doesn't approve of. I thought *this* truth was a big one because I've wondered about it all my life, and I want my brother to be a believer, too."

Faith walks over to Jane and puts her arm around her. "God doesn't force Himself on anyone. He says: 'I'm here, knocking, whenever you're willing to completely abandon your selfish ways.'" Faith asks rhetorically, "Why doesn't He reveal Himself to everyone? He cannot. It's not that He *will not*, it's because He *cannot* as long as a person stays stubborn and prideful. Pride blinds the mind and hardens the heart. Adam won't receive the Spirit before he understands that he *needs* a savior, and he begins to obey the truths that Jesus teaches us. No one can debate with God by using his or her own reasoning. From God's standpoint, our intelligence is as far below His as a rock's is below ours. We must not be disrespectful to Him. There's a passage in the Bible that tells us to work out our own salvation with fear and trembling."⁴

"And..." Simon adds, "until one receives the Holy Spirit, God's calm and quiet voice cannot be heard, nor can one understand the meaning of the Scriptures. Do you know that Jesus said a prayer just for us? He prayed to our Father, 'My prayer is not that you take them out of the world but that you protect them from the evil one...Sanctify them by the truth; your word is truth.' ⁵ "God wants us to become holy in the truth, purified, consecrated and separate from the world. Consecrate means that God sets His people apart as holy. We are *part* of this world, but we don't have to be *like* the world, and that's probably the biggest thing that the unsaved can't understand about us. They think that we are self-righteous snobs."

Jared augments Simon's words. "Dad, you know that man in church, Mr. Cooley, who sings every Sabbath a song that he has written? I heard him praying one day at Pineapple Park. He said something like this: 'Father, thank you for the miracle of your presence inside of me. I consecrate myself to you...Set me apart from the world's influence...Create a clean heart in me. I glorify you with my life.' His song the next day at church Saturday, the Sabbath, was called *Consecration*.[6]

Jared's eyes brim with sunlit sparkle. "I don't know why I can recall the words so clearly, but I liked that song very much."

David looks at Jane and she watches as he slips out the door.

David assumes that Adam is in the waiting room and he is correct. Adam stands and stares out the window so deeply in thought that he doesn't hear David come in.

It's dark outside now, but there is a full moon backlighting the stately palm trees outside. All of a sudden, a large egret alights atop the tallest tree across the street. David smiles with warm affection for the magnificent creature, and he feels tears well up in his eyes with concern for Adam as he walks over to his new friend. *Let go of my pride; let Adam see the change in me! Help him to see your truth, Lord!*

In the unseen realm, Satan sneers in defeat. He's lost another raging soul, this one belonging to David Abrams. But Adam is **mine**. I'll never let him see the truth!

In the heavens, Jesus smiles. His holy angels rejoice at the death of David's pride and rage, a transformation which God hath wrought. **Jesus reigns in David's heart.**

From Stephen's Notebook:
God has rescued us from Satan's kingdom of darkness by Christ's sacrificial death on the cross, so do away with your earthly, evil desires such as greed, anger and rage, filthy language, blaspheming (being disrespectful or using profanity) God's name, same-sex intimate relations which are detestable to God. Those who follow these and other sinful desires will not inherit the Kingdom of God. (taken from Rom 1:24-32; Lev 18:22; Gal 5:19-21; Col 3:5-8).

Endnotes

Chapter 3
1. This occurrence is true as told to the author during research for this book.

Chapter 4
1. Neal, Connie, *What's A Christian to Do with Harry Potter?* (Colorado Springs, CO: Waterbrook Press, 2001) p 71.
2. Matthew 6:29 NIV.

Chapter 5
1. A true occurrence which happened to the author in one of her many Ouija board events.
2. Robertson, Pat, *The Secret Kingdom* (Dallas, TX: Word Publishing, 1992) p 32.

Chapter 10
1. Fynn, *Mister God, This Is Anna, A True Story* (London: Collins Publishers,1974) pp 28,29.
2. Ibid, p 108.
3. Ibid, p 120.

Chapter 11
1. Luke 8:20.

Chapter 12
1. Robertson, Pat, *Miracles Can Be Yours Today* (Nashville, TN: Integrity Publishers, 2006) p 94.
2. Neal, Connie, *What's A Christian to Do with Harry Potter?* (Colorado Springs, CO: Waterbrook Press, 2001) p 90.
3. Matthew 7:13,14 NIV.
4. Neal, Connie, *What's A Christian to Do with Harry Potter?* (Colorado Springs, CO: Waterbrook Press, 2001) p 90.

Chapter 13
1. Wicca is a worldwide religion of worshiping nature and casting spells, "good" and bad. They worship creation, not the Creator.

Chapter 14
1. This was an actual event that happened to the author's dad and aunt at a séance.
2. Documented reports from Haiti and other countries that practice voodoo.
3. Psalm 23
4. Joshua 5:13,14; Revelation 1:15

Chapter 15
1. Matthew 12:30.
2. John 3:3

Chapter 17
1. John 3:1-12 NIV.

Chapter 19
1. Micah 6:8.
2. Crofton, Bill, *Florida Focus* vol. 24 (Clear Focus Productions,2008) p 14

Chapter 20
1. Neal, Connie, What's A Christian to Do with Harry Potter? (Colorado Springs, CO: Waterbrook Press, 2001) pp 24-26.
2. Copeland, Kenneth and Gloria, *From Faith to Faith Devotional* (Tulsa, OK: Harrison House, 1991, Dec 14

Chapter 21
1. Heath, Janet Field, *Little Lost Angel* (Chicago, IL: Rand McNally, 1953)
2. Finley, Mark A., *The Almost Forgotten Day* (Siloam Springs, AR: The Concerned Group, Inc. 1988.)
3. James 2:10
4. Philippians 2:12
5. John 17:15,17
6. *Consecrated* words & music by David Daniel Cooley, (LoveWalk Publishing 2008).

We invite you to view the complete
selection of titles we publish at:

www.TEACHServices.com

Scan with your mobile
device to go directly
to our website.

Please write or email us your praises, reactions, or
thoughts about this or any other book we publish at:

info@TEACHServices.com

TEACH Services, Inc.
P U B L I S H I N G

TEACH Services' titles may be purchased in bulk for
educational, business, fund-raising, or promotional use.
For more information, please e-mail:

BulkSales@TEACHServices.com

Finally, if you are interested in seeing
your own book in print, please contact us at:

publishing@TEACHServices.com

We would be happy to review your manuscript for free.

www.ingramcontent.com/pod-product-compliance
Lightning Source LLC
Chambersburg PA
CBHW060546100426
42742CB00013B/2466